PRECEPTING *in* NURSING

DEVELOPING AN EFFECTIVE WORKFORCE

SUSAN ULLRICH, EdD, MSN, RN
Professor of Nursing, Touro University Nevada
CEO, RxRN Solutions, Inc.
Professor Emeritus, California State University, Sacramento

ANN HAFFER, EdD, MSN, RN
Professor Emeritus, California State University, Sacramento

JONES AND BARTLETT PUBLISHERS
Sudbury, Massachusetts
BOSTON   TORONTO   LONDON   SINGAPORE

World Headquarters

Jones and Bartlett Publishers
40 Tall Pine Drive
Sudbury, MA 01776
978-443-5000
info@jbpub.com
www.jbpub.com

Jones and Bartlett Publishers Canada
6339 Ormindale Way
Mississauga, Ontario L5V 1J2
Canada

Jones and Bartlett Publishers International
Barb House, Barb Mews
London W6 7PA
United Kingdom

Jones and Bartlett's books and products are available through most bookstores and online booksellers. To contact Jones and Bartlett Publishers directly, call 800-832-0034, fax 978-443-8000, or visit our website www.jbpub.com.

Substantial discounts on bulk quantities of Jones and Bartlett's publications are available to corporations, professional associations, and other qualified organizations. For details and specific discount information, contact the special sales department at Jones and Bartlett via the above contact information or send an email to specialsales@jbpub.com.

The authors, editor, and publisher have made every effort to provide accurate information. However, they are not responsible for errors, omissions, or for any outcomes related to the use of the contents of this book and take no responsibility for the use of the products and procedures described. Treatments and side effects described in this book may not be applicable to all people; likewise, some people may require a dose or experience a side effect that is not described herein. Drugs and medical devices are discussed that may have limited availability controlled by the Food and Drug Administration (FDA) for use only in a research study or clinical trial. Research, clinical practice, and government regulations often change the accepted standard in this field. When consideration is being given to use of any drug in the clinical setting, the health care provider or reader is responsible for determining FDA status of the drug, reading the package insert, and reviewing prescribing information for the most up-to-date recommendations on dose, precautions, and contraindications, and determining the appropriate usage for the product. This is especially important in the case of drugs that are new or seldom used.

Production Credits
Publisher: Kevin Sullivan
Acquisitions Editor: Emily Ekle
Acquisitions Editor: Amy Sibley
Editorial Assistant: Patricia Donnelly
Associate Production Editor: Wendy Swanson
Associate Marketing Manager: Ilana Goddess
Manufacturing and Inventory Control Supervisor: Amy Bacus
Text Design and Composition: Paw Print Media
Cover Design: Brian Moore
Cover Image: © Chen Ping Hung/ShutterStock, Inc.
Printing and Binding: Courier Stoughton
Cover Printing: Courier Stoughton

Library of Congress Cataloging-in-Publication Data
Ullrich, Sue.
  Precepting in nursing : developing an effective workforce / Susan Ullrich, Ann Haffer.
      p. cm.
  Includes bibliographical references and index.
  ISBN-13: 978-0-7637-5845-5 (pbk. : alk. paper)
  ISBN-10: 0-7637-5845-0 (pbk. : alk. paper) 1. Nursing—Study and teaching (Preceptorship) I. Haffer, Ann. II. Title.
  RT74.7.U75 2009
  610.73—dc22
                              2008016975

6048

Printed in the United States of America
12 11 10 09 08   10 9 8 7 6 5 4 3 2 1

Contents

7 Maintaining Your Preceptee's Motivation   103

8 Bridging Differences: Working with Diversities   115

Introduction

The influence of each human being on others in this life is a kind of immortality.

—John Quincy Adams

PURPOSE OF THIS WORKBOOK

If you are precepting a new nurse or a student intern, you are working with a professional who is embarking on a trip that can be very stressful. New graduates are expected to function at levels they are not yet ready to achieve. They are confronted with learning many new skills and ever-increasing responsibilities. They have theoretical knowledge but limited skill proficiency. New nurses face a series of dilemmas that can be very upsetting for the new graduate. Duchscher (2001) describes difficult choices new nurses need to make, such as providing care that is effective or working to get everything done, practicing as they were taught or complying with practice standards of the "real" world, knowing they need experience but not having control over the nature of their experiences, and not wanting to jeopardize other nurses' acceptance yet needing assistance and guidance. New graduates need help while traversing these dilemmas and finding their way as they transition to practicing as professional nurses. They need guidance, support, constructive feedback, supervision, and practice opportunities that develop skill progression. In a precepted experience the new graduate or student nurse, working one-to-one with a more experienced practicing nurse, is exposed to the culture of the agency and unit along with the real-world professional roles and practices of the preceptor, self, and others.

Two shortages have prompted an increased use of precepted experiences: a shortage in nursing faculty and a shortage of professional nurses. Additionally, many hospitals are experiencing increasing nurse turnover. These issues create an ongoing need for preparing professional nurses to orient new nurses (recent graduates and nursing students), and more experienced nurses who are changing places of employment (American Association of Colleges of Nursing, 2005).

After more than 20 years of working with precepted experiences in schools of nursing, the authors, having learned many lessons about the process, decided to write a workbook that would be a resource for nurses about to embark on a precepting journey.

Each chapter builds essential preceptor knowledge and skills. The content of the workbook is most useful for nurses seeking to enhance their development as a preceptor when working with nursing students, new graduates, or experienced nurses. Hospitals could use this workbook to provide the foundation for their preceptor programs as they prepare staff nurses for precepting roles. Schools of nursing could use this workbook to augment staff nurse preceptor role development for those nurses who have been selected as academic preceptors.

Precepting Leads to Giving and Getting

Congratulations!

You are considering or have already agreed to become a preceptor for a nurse or nursing student. Thank you and congratulations! You were likely selected because of your skills and experience; your ability to inspire, coach, advise, and model sound clinical behaviors; and your leadership among your team of peers. Just think! In your role as preceptor, you can contribute to the development of a professional nurse, a colleague you will want as a team member. Surely you want a worker who performs safely, responsibly, and effectively. You have an opportunity to "grow" this kind of nurse. As the quote at the beginning of the introduction suggests, helping new employees and students get sound starts in professional nursing leads to their carrying parts of your exemplary model into their practices.

Why Your Contribution Is Valued

Both you and your preceptee will experience many benefits from the precepting experience. For you, it can be a time of personal growth and professional clarification as you work with your preceptee in problem solving, assisting in analyzing subtle differences in patient responses to illness, and making decisions about therapeutic interventions. It can be gratifying for you to participate in your preceptee's professional development. You will likely get satisfaction knowing you have helped a fellow professional get a sound start and at the same time improved your own skills (Lenners, Wilson, Connor, & Fenton, 2006). In addition to your personal satisfaction, you will receive recognition from your peers and other healthcare professionals for your contributions and commitment to the nursing profession.

For the preceptee, research on the benefits of precepted experiences describes improved problem-solving and critical thinking skills, increased application of theory to practice, positive changes in role expectations and self-image, less reality shock when entering the work force, and improved sense of clinical competence and self-confidence

(Myrick, 2002; Myrick & Yonge, 2004; Scheetz, 1989; Spence Laschinger & MacMaster, 1992; Yonge & Trojan, 1992).

Your preceptee will benefit from your guidance and from sharing your valuable clinical experiences. Working with you will solidify your preceptee's values and beliefs about nursing, provide many opportunities for applying nursing practice standards in your clinical setting, and foster acceptance of your preceptee within your work group. Because of you, your preceptee will begin to know what it is like to be a nurse, to think like a nurse, and to work as a valuable team member. When you provide a supportive environment, you have an immense influence in helping your preceptee comfortably make the stressful trip from student or new graduate to professional nurse (Delaney, 2003). If your preceptee is experienced, you will primarily influence a smooth transition to specifics in your agency and on your unit.

Research findings support that you not only influence your preceptee's transition into practice, when your precepting is effective you also are more likely to have an effect on staff nurse retention (Alvarez, 1993; Andersen, 1989; Atkins & Williams, 1995; Lenners et al., 2006). The U.S. shortage of registered nurses is expected to increase to 340,000 by the year 2020 (Auerbach, Buerhaus, & Staiger, 2007). In one study looking at the retention of 3,266 newly licensed nurses, reasons cited for leaving their first job included poor management (42%), stressful work conditions (37%), and wanting to get experience in a different clinical area (34%). Retention in today's nursing workforce is critical. Statistics describe 35% to 61% of new graduates change their first agency employer or leave the profession of nursing within their first year (Aiken, Clarke, Sloane, & Sochalski, 2001). The ability to retain nurses is related to increasingly intense work environments that create significant stress for new nurses and affect job satisfaction. Dissatisfied nurses are likely to leave their positions (Ulrich et al., 2006). Grindel (2004, p. 37) suggested that, "Mentorship programs are essential strategies to retain novice nurses in clinical practice as they begin their evolution as professional nurses." The cost of orienting a new employee, particularly a new nurse or an immigrated nurse, is considerable. After you and your preceptee have invested considerable time and effort, surely you and your organization want to retain this nurse. It's important to create an optimal supportive work environment to help new nurses feel valued and less overwhelmed, reduce new-nurse stresses, and ultimately have a positive effect on retention rates (Carroll, 2005; Kovner, 2007).

How Does This Workbook Facilitate Effective Precepting Experiences?

The return of your substantial efforts is significant for retaining nurses, for sound preceptee professional development, and for achieving quality health care. These are awesome responsibilities; however, this workbook is designed to facilitate your transition to being an effective preceptor. Thorough preparation for the preceptor role is the key to successful precepting processes (Gaberson & Oermann, 2007). The chapters guide you through the process by providing information and strategies to assist you to effectively coach and facilitate a new nurse's integration into your healthcare organization and into the profession of nursing.

How Do the Roles of Precepting Differ from Those of Mentoring?

The terms *mentoring* and *precepting* are frequently used interchangeably; however, there are some differences between the two roles. Much of the literature describes many behaviors that are shared by both the mentor and preceptor. Those roles involve one-to-one relationships and include numerous supportive roles such as teaching, coaching, advocating, role modeling, supporting, guiding, supervising, facilitating, and guiding (Gaberson & Oermann, 2007; Morton-Cooper & Palmer, 2000; Myrick & Yonge, 2003; Yonge, Billay, Myrick, & Luhanga, 2007). There are, however, a few distinct differences in the two roles.

- Precepting usually occurs in a clinical situation focused on professional development, often a student or new graduate, whereas mentoring may include a relationship beyond the professional setting.

- Precepting is usually limited to a few weeks or months. The process is more specifically focused on given objectives and educational settings, whereas mentoring tends to be an ongoing long-term relationship involving shared goal setting in a variety of situations.

- Preceptors are usually assigned to a preceptee. Neither chooses the other. Mentors and mentees generally have a mutual agreement to engage in the process. The relationship tends to evolve over time.

- Formal evaluation occurs at specified times during a precepted experience, but this is not as structured in the mentoring situation. Although the mentor evaluates and shares observations about the mentee's behaviors, the process is guided by events occurring in the situation.

- Precepting generally involves orienting a nurse just starting a career or a new position. Mentoring can occur anytime during a career.

You may become both a preceptor and a mentor. Though you start out being an appointed preceptor, your relationship with your preceptee may continue beyond the designated precepted orientation and may evolve into more of the characteristics of a mentoring relationship.

Objectives

After completing the workbook and related learning activities, you should be able to

1. Describe the roles and responsibilities of all participants involved in the precepted experience.

2. Describe the roles and responsibilities of the preceptor and preceptee.

3. Describe legal and regulatory controls that influence the precepting process.

4. During the precepting process, implement practices prescribed by legal and regulatory controls.

5. Develop and implement a comprehensive orientation plan for a preceptee.

6. Describe beginner behaviors observed in the assigned preceptee.

7. Describe your own level of expertise in the range from competent to expert practitioner level.

8. Describe strategies for working with beginner behaviors to facilitate preceptee skill progression.

9. Develop and use strategies to facilitate preceptee's time management skill progression.

10. Describe preceptor strategies that apply adult learning principles.

11. Describe preceptor approaches that facilitate preceptee learning styles.

12. Describe preceptor approaches to enhance motivation and performance.

13. Use a simplified model of cultural congruence to develop preceptor development strategies that demonstrate cultural congruence with your preceptee's needs.

14. Complete a cultural assessment of your organization's culture.

15. Develop cultural awareness, knowledge, and skills when working with your preceptee.

16. Develop strategies for working with preceptees who are from a different generation.

17. Develop strategies for working with internationally educated nurses.

18. Describe preceptor roles in the processes of continuous assessment.

19. Complete a self-assessment of your progress in your preceptor role.

Approaches Used in Each Chapter

Objectives

Objectives are given at the beginning of each chapter to help you focus on what we hope you will learn after completing the chapter activities. Review them again when you finish the chapter and decide if you have achieved the intended outcomes.

Questions to Guide Your Learning

Following the objectives, you are asked several questions designed to stimulate and focus your interest in the chapter concepts that we hope influence how you apply them in your precepting practices. The questions ask you to reflect about the most important factors you will be learning. At the end of the chapter we ask you to answer these questions. Appendix A offers suggested answers to these questions.

Chapter Focus

Following the chapter objectives and questions, concepts and learning activities are presented about preceptor knowledge, skills, and strategies critical to effective precepting. One could say the chapters represent 10 steps to effective precepting. See the following brief chapter descriptions.

Preceptor Strategies Focused on Facilitating Skill Progression in the Chapter Topic

For each of the concepts in the chapters several related preceptor strategies are suggested. These strategies are applications of the knowledge and skills discussed in the chapters. For example, in one chapter we talk about time management, which is a major problem for new nurses. Several strategies are suggested for helping the preceptee develop good time management.

Though the primary focus of this workbook is on strategies for working with newly graduated nurses employed by healthcare agencies and student nurse interns from schools of nursing, we also include alternatives when precepting a more experienced nurse. However, many of the preceptor strategies suggested for new nurses also apply when working with more experienced nurses, particularly if these nurses are changing to agencies and units that are very different from their previous clinical experiences. Though we describe strategies related to the chapter topics, there may be variations you need to make due to hospital or nursing school policies and procedures.

Reflection

Each chapter offers opportunities to engage in reflective activities. Reflective strategies may include discussions, developing answers to questions about situations, writing about experiences in journals or logs, sharing stories, and analyzing ways to improve and repeat behaviors. Although experiences encountered during the precepting process are an essential ingredient for learning, experience alone is not sufficient for learning. Reflection about experiences to create meaning from them leads to and enhances learning. Thinking about experiences gives access to and constructs meaning from past experience (Cohen, 2005). Reflection also enhances memory for past experiences that can be applied to new similar experiences. It involves cognitive processes such as noting phenomena, similarities, differences, and patterns; exploring possibilities; asking and answering questions; challenging and analyzing assumptions; making decisions about actions; and connecting past experiences with current events (Atkins & Murphy, 1993; Tanner, 2006).

Chapter Summary

Each chapter ends with a brief summary of the concepts and strategies included in the chapter.

Forms That Guide Preceptee and Preceptor

Most of the chapters include forms designed to guide and enhance learning, such as anecdotal note forms, a checklist of beginner behaviors, or a cultural assessment guide. When the chapter includes forms they appear at the end of the chapter.

Overview of Chapters

Chapter 1 focuses on describing the roles of all participants involved in the precepting process: the preceptor, preceptee, nursing administration, nursing education, and unit manager. All involved need to know their roles as well as the roles of others if the experience is going to be effective.

Chapter 2 turns to legal and regulatory controls you should consider before starting and throughout a precepting experience. Examples include immunizations your preceptee should have, state regulations for preceptor qualifications, contracts when working with students, and liability concerns, among several other considerations.

Chapter 3 should get you off to a good start with planning for orientation and ways to map out how you and the preceptee progress in skill development.

Because you will most likely be working with a beginner (even though your preceptee has had previous experience), Chapter 4 describes classic beginner behaviors and ways of dealing with them so that skill progression moves along smoothly.

Chapter 5 concentrates on strategies that facilitate progression in time management skills. When one is new to a situation, it is difficult to anticipate how long it takes to complete various activities. Because of a lack of experience, it is also a problem to anticipate events that take time; therefore unexpected events interfere with efficient organization.

Chapter 6 describes principles and assumptions about adult learners along with strategies of using them with adult learners. The chapter also deals with learning styles. You may learn very easily by just hearing some verbal directions, whereas your preceptee may need to see the directions or may need to have hands-on experience to learn. You and your preceptee have preferred learning styles. Ways of working with preceptee styles are suggested.

Chapter 7 explores ways of maintaining motivation. Motivation is a critical factor for facilitating skill progression and professional socialization. Factors that influence motivation as well as preceptor strategies that tend to motivate are addressed in this chapter.

Chapter 8 introduces you to ways of thinking about and working with diversities. You will learn the importance of assessing organizational culture and explore a model for developing culturally congruent skills to enable you to work more effectively with a preceptee who is generationally or educationally different from you.

How well you and your preceptee are progressing is addressed in Chapter 9. Guidelines for assessing your preceptee are described. It is very important to keep track of improvements as well as needed changes. How you assess and offer feedback can significantly influence a successful precepting experience. Suggestions are offered for providing consistent, structured, constructive, and goal-oriented feedback and guidance.

Chapter 10 summarizes key preceptor strategies for each chapter. The chapter also describes potential precepting problems and suggests potential strategies for responding to these problems.

References

Aiken, L. H., Clarke, S. P., Sloane, D. M., & Sochalski, J. (2001). An international perspective on hospital nurses' work environments: The case for reform. *Policy, Politics, & Nursing Practice, 2,* 253–261.

Alvarez, E. (1993). Mentoring undergraduate ethnic minority students: A strategy for retention. *Journal of Nursing Education, 32,* 230–232.

American Association of Colleges of Nursing. (2005). *Faculty shortages in baccalaureate and graduate nursing programs: Scope of problems and strategies for expanding the supply.* Retrieved February 27, 2008, from http://www.aacn.nche.edu/Publications/WhitePapers/FacultyShortages.htm

Andersen, S. L. (1989). The nurse advocate project: A strategy to retain new graduates. *Journal of Nursing Administration, 19,* 22–26.

Atkins, S., & Murphy, K. (1993). Reflection: A review of the literature. *Journal of Advanced Nursing, 18,* 1188–1192.

Atkins, S., & Williams, A. (1995). Registered nurses' experiences of mentoring undergraduate nursing students. *Journal of Advanced Nursing, 21*(5), 1006–1015.

Auerbach, D., Buerhaus, P., & Staiger, D. (2007). Better late than never: Workforce supply implications of later entry into nursing. *Health Affairs, 26,* 178–185.

Carroll, T. I. (2005). Stressful life events among new nurses: Implications for retaining new graduates. *Nursing Administration Quarterly, 29,* 292–296.

Cohen, J. (2005). The mirror as metaphor for the reflective practitioner. In M. H. Oermann & K. T. Heinrich (Eds.), *Annual review of nursing education: Vol. 3. Strategies for teaching, assessment, and program planning* (pp. 313–330). New York: Springer.

Delaney, C. (2003). Walking a fine line: Graduate nurses' transition experiences during orientation. *Journal of Nursing Education, 41,* 437–443.

Duchscher, J. E. B. (2001). Out in the real world: Newly graduated nurses in acute care speak out. *Journal of Nursing Administration, 31,* 426–439.

Gaberson, K. B., & Oermann, M. H. (Eds.). (2007). *Clinical teaching strategies in nursing* (2nd ed.). New York: Springer.

Grindel, C. G. (2004). Mentorship: A key to retention and recruitment. *Medical and Surgical Nursing, 13,* 36–37.

Kovner, C. T. (2007). Newly licensed RNs' characteristics, work attitudes, and intentions to work. *American Journal of Nursing, 109,* 58.

Lenners, D. W., Wilson, V. W., Connor, P., & Fenton, J. (2006). Mentorship: Increasing retention probabilities. *Journal of Nursing Administration, 14,* 652–654.

Morton-Cooper, A., & Palmer, A. (2000). *Mentoring, preceptorship and clinical supervision: A guide to professional support roles in clinical practice* (2nd ed.). Malden, MA: Blackwell Science.

Myrick, F. (2002). Preceptorship and critical thinking in nursing education. *Journal of Nursing Education, 41,* 154–164.

Myrick, F., & Yonge, O. (2003) Preceptorship: A quintessential component of nursing education. In M. H. Oermann & K. T. Heinrich (Eds.), *Annual review of nursing education* (Vol. 1, pp. 91–108). New York: Springer.

Myrick, F., & Yonge, O. (2004). Enhancing critical thinking in the preceptorship experience in nursing education. *Journal of Advanced Nursing, 45,* 371–380.

Scheetz, L. J. (1989). Baccalaureate nursing student preceptorship programs and the development of clinical competence. *Journal of Nursing Education, 28,* 29–35.

Spence Laschinger, H. K., & MacMaster, E. (1992). Effect of pregraduate preceptorship experience on development of adaptive competencies of baccalaureate nursing students. *Journal of Nursing Education, 31,* 258–264.

Tanner, C. A., (2006). Thinking like a nurse: A research-based model of clinical judgment in nursing. *Journal of Nursing Education, 45,* 204–211.

Ulrich, B. T., Lavandero, R., Hart, K., Woods, D., Lettett, J., & Taylor, D. (2006). Critical care nurses' work environments: A baseline status report. *Critical Care Nurse, 26,* 46–57.

Yonge., O., Billay, D., Myrick, F., & Luhanga, F. (2007). Preceptorship and mentorship: Not merely a matter of semantics. *International Journal of Nursing Education Scholarship, 4*(1), Article 19.

Yonge, O., & Trojan, L. (1992). The nursing performance of preceptored and non-preceptored baccalaureate nursing students. *The Canadian Journal of Nursing Research, 24*(2), 61–75.

About the Authors

SUSAN ULLRICH

Susan Ullrich earned her BSN from the University of Nevada Orvis School of Nursing in 1976. She worked in oncology, medical-surgical, postpartum, and pediatrics as an acute care nurse. Before earning her MSN from California State University Sacramento (CSUS), Dr. Ullrich held administrative positions in nursing. She graduated from CSUS with an MSN in nursing education and administration after which she began her teaching career. Her primary teaching responsibilities included courses in administration and education, and she coordinated precepted experiences for more than 250 nursing students each semester. In 1997, Dr. Ullrich earned her EdD in educational leadership and curriculum development from the University of Southern California. In 2005, Dr. Ullrich worked with Touro University in Henderson, Nevada to start the state's first private nursing school. She designed and implemented their Entry Level Master's, RN-MSN, and BSN-MSN programs. In 2006, Dr. Ullrich launched RxRN Solutions, Inc., an educational company that focuses on transitioning internationally educated nurses into professional practice in the United States. Dr. Ullrich's research agenda focuses on role socialization of beginners and of culturally diverse nurses.

ANN HAFFER

Ann Haffer earned her BSN and MSN from Ohio State University, in 1960 and 1961 respectively, and an EdD from the University of San Francisco with a concentration in curriculum and instruction in 1990. Dr. Haffer taught nursing for 40 years. She started teaching nursing fundamentals and leadership as an instructor at Ohio State University. She taught in and coordinated medical-surgical nursing at Incarnate Word College in San Antonio for 6 years. As an assistant professor she taught and coordinated medical-surgical nursing at Midwestern State University, Wichita Falls, Texas for 5 years. From 1976 to 1979, while accompanying her husband on a tour of duty in

Germany, Dr. Haffer was the American Red Cross Nursing Chairman and School Health Educator in the Department of Defense schools in Bitburg, Germany. From 1979 until retiring as professor emeritus in 2006, Dr. Haffer remained at California State University, Sacramento, teaching courses in leadership and management and clinical diagnostic reasoning in the undergraduate program and research and educational program development courses in the graduate program. From 1989 to 2001 she served as Associate Director of the Division of Nursing at CSUS. During her tenure at CSUS she served on the University Faculty Senate as chairman of the Curriculum Committee and as the Assessment Coordinator for the university. In 1990, Dr. Haffer received an Excellence in Teaching award from the local chapter of Sigma Theta Tau International. In 2002, the California State University, Sacramento College of Health and Human Services awarded her the Outstanding Service Award for service to the university. Dr. Haffer's primary area of research and publication has focused on beginner nurses' behaviors, and ways of working with these behaviors, and on clinical reasoning/critical thinking development in beginning nurses.

CHAPTER ONE

What Everyone Should Be Doing: Roles and Responsibilities

You cannot hope to build a better world without improving the individuals. To that end each of us must work for his own improvement, and at the same time share a general responsibility for all humanity, our particular duty being to aid those to whom we think we can be most useful.

—Marie Curie 1867–1934

INTRODUCTION

In your role as preceptor you are in a position to "aid those to whom we think we can be most useful." To effectively do so, each formal participant in the plan for your preceptee's development must be cognizant of role responsibilities and functions. To achieve in these is to provide a solid foundation of support for your preceptee.

As you become familiar with who is responsible for what, organizing your preceptee's day is accomplished with greater clarity and depth, adding to the quality of the experience. The purpose of this chapter is to describe the roles of the manager or charge nurse, the preceptor, the preceptee, and the faculty member (if the preceptee is a student nurse), to give you tools to help you organize your preceptee's day, and to provide an introductory discussion about preceptee evaluation. Three worksheets, the Preceptor Planning Guide, the Preceptor Progress Journal, and the Preceptee Reflective Journal, are discussed and copies of each are provided at the end of this chapter.

OBJECTIVES

After completing the chapter and related learning activities, you should be able to

1. Describe the roles and responsibilities of the preceptee.
2. Describe the roles and responsibilities of the unit manager or charge nurse.
3. Describe the roles and responsibilities of the preceptor.

4. Describe the roles and responsibilities of the faculty member if the preceptee is a student nurse.

5. Use the Preceptor Planning Guide when planning for your preceptee's daily experiences.

6. Describe a plan of intervention if you and your preceptee are experiencing difficulties.

7. Describe ways in which you can help your preceptee use reflection as a strategy for knowledge development and integration.

QUESTIONS TO GUIDE YOUR LEARNING

1. Are you able to identify the participants who are facilitating your preceptee's experiences?

2. Do you know the roles and responsibilities of each of the participants?

3. What are the roles and responsibilities of the preceptor?

4. How will you help your preceptee maximize learning experiences when planning for daily activities?

5. Why meet with your preceptee at the end of the shift/workday? What will you talk about?

6. How will you respond if you believe you are not a "good match" for your preceptee?

7. What is the purpose of your preceptee's reflective journal?

8. Why is reflective journaling an effective strategy for maximizing learning?

9. Is it appropriate to share your preceptee's reflective journal with your colleagues?

10. Who is responsible for evaluating the employee preceptee?

Roles and Responsibilities

Knowing how each participant fits into the whole picture of your preceptee's learning experience is essential for your role development as a preceptor. Knowing the roles, responsibilities, and potential contributions of each formal member of your preceptee's learning plan facilitates a smooth learning experience for your preceptee and minimizes duplication and reduces confusion. So, let's begin with your roles and your responsibilities as the preceptor.

What You Should Be Doing as a Preceptor

Your role as preceptor is multifaceted and includes the roles of coach, teacher, facilitator, resource person, and evaluator. At first glance you might be rethinking your willingness or your ability to assume the role of preceptor. Remember the purpose of this workbook and continue reading. You have been selected to participate in this role or you have volunteered to do so because you believe you have something to offer either a student nurse, a new nurse, or an experienced nurse who will be orienting with you. So, let's take an in-depth look at each component of your preceptor role.

Your Role as Coach

A coach directs and guides a learner. In your case you will be directing and guiding your preceptee's learning experiences. You will

1. Meet with your preceptee initially and throughout the experience at predetermined times to establish, review, and evaluate objectives and activities in addition to the daily contact that you will have with your preceptee.

2. Jointly, in collaboration with your preceptee and others as needed, strategize and arrange assignments, projects, and activities designed to meet your preceptee's learning objectives. Implementing and evaluating these learning strategies within a designated time frame provides structure to the overall plan for learning achievement and ensures relevant feedback through assessment of objective achievement.

3. Encourage your preceptee to be self-directed. As your preceptee progresses, it is important that you allow for self-direction. Your role will change from that of leader to a more supportive role as your preceptee develops professionally, moving toward independence. An in-depth discussion of how your preceptee develops professionally is found in Chapter 4.

Your Role as Teacher

A teacher manages the learning possibilities and opportunities provided by a variety of learning experiences. In this case you will be seeking experiences to enhance learning. Initially, you might find "introductory" experiences that allow a beginner to build on current knowledge. Likewise, if you are precepting an experienced nurse you will

1. Arrange for learning experiences that build on the nurse's knowledge. An effective strategy to use with a student preceptee might be finding a breast-feeding class for new moms and creating time for your preceptee to attend the class. Similarly, when precepting an experienced nurse who is new to women's health, you might assign your preceptee to work with an experienced labor and delivery nurse who is providing care to a high-risk mother.

2. Share your experiences and knowledge with the preceptee to develop the preceptee's abilities and confidence. In this role you may provide resources to support the needs of your preceptee. To facilitate learning, encourage your preceptee to reflect on experiences. Demonstrate techniques, provide examples, and encourage questioning and discussion.

Your Role as Facilitator

As a facilitator you will help to bring about an outcome through guidance and supervision. In this case the outcome is an optimal learning experience. You are knowledgeable about structure, the routines, and the protocols occurring in your unit. Use this knowledge to help your preceptee gain a global overview of how things operate. Call on other healthcare team members to provide learning opportunities that are relevant to the plan you and your preceptee set forth. Use your knowledge and influence to remove obstacles so that learning opportunities are enhanced. Help your preceptee integrate into the work group by making introductions and ensuring your preceptee knows "how things are done."

Your Role as a Resource Person

In your role as resource person you will help your preceptee discover the people, equipment, or material used to perform a project or a task. To maximize learning, your preceptee needs to know the people, place, or thing to accomplish objectives. Help your preceptee develop a network by introducing nurses and ancillary staff who provide care to the constituency of clients on your unit. Assist your preceptee in learning the policies and procedures that guide professional practice. Help your preceptee find the necessary equipment to complete a procedure or a task. Facilitate discovery of who, what, when, where, and why so that your preceptee becomes an asset to the organization and a valued colleague. Chapter 3 offers additional suggestions to help you facilitate your preceptee's entrée into your work culture.

Your Role as Evaluator

As an evaluator you have the responsibility of assessing your preceptee's level of progress in achieving objectives. If you are precepting a new nurse or an experienced nurse, you have the added responsibility of assessing the effectiveness of your collaborative plan for your preceptee's orientation to your organization. You will be responsible for

1. Giving your preceptee feedback about performance and progress on an ongoing basis.
2. Evaluating your preceptee's level of achievement in meeting objectives.
3. Participating in joint conferences with your preceptee and the unit manager (if preceptee is a new hire) or joint conferences with your student preceptee and the faculty liaison as scheduled.
4. Ensuring that your preceptee conducts an ongoing self-evaluation.
5. Evaluating your role as preceptor in collaboration with your preceptee.

In summary, you have, at some point, demonstrated exceptional nursing care delivery, efficient organizational skills, and effective communication with your colleagues and with patients. These are skills that provide a solid foundation for your development as a preceptor. *Your primary roles, then, are to serve as a clinical expert, a role model for professional behavior, and to provide direct supervision of your preceptee* as you teach, facilitate, provide resources, and evaluate your preceptee's progress.

What Your Preceptee Should be Doing

To fully embrace your role as a preceptor, you must understand the behaviors and responsibilities of your preceptee. You may want to expand the roles and responsibilities of your preceptee depending on the nature of your relationship with the student, new employee, or experienced nurse. Please take time to review these basic behaviors and responsibilities with your preceptee to minimize the occurrence of misunderstandings and to maximize productivity of your preceptor–preceptee relationship. In addition to the given objectives of the precepted experience, your preceptee should

1. *Analyze and determine the priorities for the experience.* You might query your preceptee about individual objectives of the experience. In collaboration with you, elaboration and prioritization of specific learning objectives should be clearly articulated in writing. Discuss reciprocal expectations and devise a tentative schedule of activities to meet the identified learning objectives. You may want to include the unit manager in this process, especially if your preceptee is a new employee.

2. *Seek your supervision and feedback on an ongoing basis.* Scheduling an initial conference and subsequent weekly conferences for the purpose of reviewing and reevaluating the learning objectives enables your preceptee to maintain a productive focus for learning achievement. Allow your preceptee to plan the agenda for these conferences.

3. *Maintain a daily log that reflects a synthesis of learning experiences for the week.* A detailed description of the learning log and rationale for why such a strategy is used is discussed in Chapter 3.

4. *Perform in a role that is consistent with the administrative framework of your organization.* You may need to help your preceptee identify the framework. Your preceptee is responsible for providing required documentation such as evidence of professional liability insurance, cardiopulmonary resuscitation certificate, evidence of having been immunized, and other forms of evidence as required by your organization. Your human resources department can provide you with a detailed list of required documents.

5. *Inform you of problems that arise during the experience.* You should also be informed of illness or emergencies that preclude any prearranged commitments for the experience.

6. *Conduct a self-evaluation as measured against the clinical objectives or the job description.* In addition, the preceptor may be responsible for completing a formal assessment of the preceptee's experience as defined by organizational policy.

7. *Provide safe and effective nursing care to selected clients while meeting the objectives of the experience.* In doing so your preceptee should maintain communication with you and other agency personnel to ensure continuity of care. If your organization has additional requirements of your preceptee, share these requirements both verbally and in writing. Doing so ensures transparency of the relationship and maximizes the potential for achievement of your preceptee's learning outcomes.

What the Faculty Liaison Should be Doing

If your preceptee is a student, you need to be aware of common roles and responsibilities of the faculty liaison. The faculty liaison is responsible for supervising an individual student's experience. Most faculty liaisons are responsible for:

1. *Initiating contact with the preceptor.* At this initial meeting expect to receive a copy of the course description, learning objectives, beginning and ending dates of the precepted experience, and the number of hours required to fulfill the objectives.

2. *Maintaining communication* with you to clarify student, instructor, and agency roles, to validate learning objectives, and to facilitate and monitor the student's precepted experience.

3. *Meeting with the student on a regular basis* to provide the student supervision for achieving learning objectives and to facilitate progression. These meetings usually occur on campus and are organized as a seminar session in which several students come together to share their experiences. Usually you are not expected to attend these seminars, but your presence could be an added benefit.

4. *Reviewing the student's daily log at least every week to provide timely feedback.* Information written in the student log is held in confidence. Although it is not a requirement, some preceptors learn more about the preceptee's thinking from reading the student's log. If you choose to do so, seek permission from the student.

5. *Sharing contact information with you that includes e-mail address, office phone number, and off-hours contact information.* The faculty liaison is usually available to you for consultation on a 24-hour basis. Expect the faculty liaison to make periodic visits to your organization to participate in joint conferences with the student and you. Periodic contact may occur via telephone conference if the precepting experience is located at a distance.

6. *Providing contact information for a substitute liaison* in the event the faculty liaison has a change in availability.

7. *Completing final assessments and formal evaluations.* Providing reliable and valid data is a responsibility that should be shared by all participants in your preceptee's learning experience. The faculty liaison completes an evaluation of the student assessing achievement of the stated learning objectives using the form provided by the school of nursing. The final evaluation is a synthesis of the collaborative input of all the other participants. Usually, assessment data are gathered through an evaluation conference with the preceptor and the student at the end of the semester.

This discussion of faculty responsibilities is generated from the expectations of performance from several schools of nursing. You might discover the faculty role to be more or less complex. The minimum information that must be shared with you is the faculty liaison contact information.

What the Manager Should be Doing

Involvement of the unit or department manager varies with the requirements of the position within each organization. The level of manager participation will be greater if your preceptee is a new employee. If that is the case, you would anticipate that the unit or department manager would:

1. *Identify qualified preceptors.* More than likely you were approached by your manager to precept either a student or a new employee. Your manager has knowledge of your ability to teach and communicate and knows of your level of competence as a nurse.

2. *Support you in providing clinical experiences necessary to meet your preceptee's learning objectives.* The manager can facilitate your preceptee's entrée into other departments through communication at the managerial level, creating a seamless and comprehensive learning experience.

3. *Participate in the evaluation of the total preceptor program.* Generally, the manager's role is minimized if your preceptee is a student. If that is the case, you might find that your manger is identified as the agency contact person who is responsible for coordinating student placement in the preceptor program. The manager's role extends to identify and assign qualified preceptors and to participate in the evaluation of the program at the end of the academic year.

Let these role descriptions be guides. Some participant roles and responsibilities may be expanded or minimized depending on the preceptor program. If you have any problems or questions, meet with your manager or clinical educator for assistance.

Preceptor Strategies

Working with the Beginning Nurse

1. Meet with your preceptee and the faculty liaison, if your preceptee is a student, to assess the preceptee's learning experience. Assess the preceptee's learning goals and the course objectives. Are they achievable in the length of time you will be working together?

2. Encourage your preceptee to keep a reflective journal of experiences. This is a useful strategy for helping your preceptee integrate new knowledge and provides insight for you as you read and provide focusing comments. A template for preceptee reflection (**Form 1-2**) is included.

3. Students are precepted at differing levels of their academic education. If your agency clinically supports various schools of nursing, validate your preceptee's level of education and experience. Discuss limitations in the student preceptee's practice. Are there skills the student preceptee is not allowed to perform?

4. Call on your colleagues to provide learning opportunities that are relevant to your preceptee's clinical goals.

5. Welcome your preceptee to your unit. Enthusiastically introduce your preceptee to your workgroup network (nurses and ancillary staff). Share the preceptee's level of education and any limitations of practice.

6. You have the responsibility of assessing your preceptee's level of achievement in meeting learning objectives. There is a tendency to evaluate the preceptee as "the best I've ever had." It is important to provide constructive assessment feedback that will

help your preceptee develop professionally. Be honest, be direct, and be encouraging. You may use the Preceptor Planning Guide (**Form 1-1**) to plan and assess your preceptee's progress.

7. Provide your student preceptee with frequent feedback. Critically analyze your preceptee's achievement in meeting objectives. Take time to share your impressions with your preceptee. Ongoing feedback is essential for maximizing learning experiences. Collaboration will help you to better understand how your preceptee is developing professionally. Consult with the faculty liaison and the student preceptee if refinement of the objectives is in order.

8. It is your responsibility to ensure that your preceptee is performing in a role that is consistent with the administrative framework of your organization. Make certain that all forms, documents, and evaluations are kept on file with the appropriate department.

9. Maintain ongoing communication with the faculty liaison regarding student progress. Keep the faculty liaison informed of potential or real problems.

10. Maintain accurate contact information for both the student and the faculty liaison. This should include e-mail address, cell phone number, office phone number, and off-hours contact information. If the faculty liaison is unavailable, be certain you have the contact information for the substitute liaison and the administrative contact for the school of nursing. Exchange your contact information with both the student and the faculty liaison.

11. Keep your manager informed about the progress of the precepted learning experience. Provide feedback when asked to evaluate the preceptor program. Be honest and provide clear objective examples.

12. The Preceptor Progress Journal (**Form 1-3**) offers you an opportunity to reflect on your experiences as a preceptor. Reflection is an integral component of teaching and learning. When you reflect on past experiences, the process provides you with the opportunity to review scenarios and allows you to review your involvement in the scenario. When you take time to reflect, you can replay the scenario and rehearse different interactions and behaviors that might yield differing outcomes. You can make hypothetical changes that allow you to learn from the past and prepare to be better equipped to manage new and similar situations. If you choose to keep a journal of your experiences as a preceptor, you will see your progress as you develop in your role.

Working with the Experienced Nurse

The following are strategies that may be useful when working with an experienced nurse who is orienting on your unit.

1. Meet with your preceptee to collaboratively determine the outcomes of the precepted experience. When working with an experienced nurse, you may want to be more

supportive than directive in your preceptor role. In this case you will be facilitating learning experiences by seeking experiences that enhance learning.

2. Plan experiences that build on the preceptee's knowledge. Encourage your preceptee to be self-directed. Support your preceptee's professional development by providing frequent feedback.

3. Share your knowledge of the organization's structure, routines, and protocols. Use this knowledge to help your experienced preceptee learn how things are done. Introduce your preceptee to your colleagues.

4. Evaluate your preceptee's achievement in meeting experience objectives. Conduct joint conferences with the manager and preceptee in an effort to maximize progress. Solve problems as they arise.

5. Help your preceptee self-analyze professional progress. Your organization may provide a formal evaluation form. In addition, you may want to use the Preceptor Planning Guide (**Form 1-1**) to track your preceptee's progress.

6. Just as when working with the student preceptee, use reflection to enhance both your learning as a preceptor and your preceptee's learning experiences. You may want to use the Preceptor Progress Journal (**Form 1-3**) to reflect on your progress as a preceptor. Your preceptee may want to use the Preceptee Reflective Journal (**Form 1-2**) as a tool for reflection.

7. You might be one of a group of preceptors who are precepting both students and new employees. Your organization may want to initiate an institutional Web log ("blog") that would allow you to communicate your experiences with each other using an online format. Sharing your experiences and challenges can be a useful method of collaborative support and may facilitate your learning. See Trafford (2005) for a comprehensive discussion of how to set up an institutional blog and on the application of reflection as a process for learning.

Summary

Knowing the roles and responsibilities of each participant helps you manage your preceptee's learning experience. Thinking of ways you can facilitate your preceptee's development and using the Preceptor Planning Guide may facilitate your preceptee's success. You may want to assess the progress of your preceptee by encouraging the use of the Preceptee Reflective Journal. Finally, you may want to reflect on and share your experiences as a preceptor with others who are preceptors within your organization using the Preceptor Progress Journal or by discussing your experiences on a blog.

Reflection

- Refer to the section in the beginning of this chapter called Questions to Guide your Learning. After completing this chapter see if you can answer the questions. Some suggested answers are included in Appendix A.

- Begin a journal of your experiences. Reflect about how you are going to "aid those to whom we think we can be most useful."

- Are you able to list the people who are facilitating your preceptee's experiences?

- In your role as facilitator, what two things can you do to help your preceptee learn the structure of the workday?

- When working with students you are required to keep copies of your preceptee's health clearances. What documents should you collect from your preceptee and where are the copies kept?

- You find that your nurse coworkers are very enthusiastic about having a preceptee on the floor. As a professional "character building strategy" the coworkers frequently delegate tasks and skills to your preceptee. Is this acceptable? If not, how will you manage this situation?

- How will you use your preceptee's reflective journal to enhance professional progression?

- What is the value of the Preceptor Progress Journal in your professional development as a preceptor?

- Your coworkers provide you with written notes evaluating your preceptee's progression. How will you use the notes?

- You need to speak with the faculty liaison, but after 2 days of trying you're unable to reach him. What will you do?

References

Trafford, P. (2005). *Mobile blogs, personal reflections and learning environments.* Retrieved February 19, 2008, from http://www.ariadne.ac.uk/issue44/trafford/

NOTES

FORM 1-1: PRECEPTOR PLANNING GUIDE

Complete this form in collaboration with your preceptee each time you work together. It is necessary for you to track progress. Use this form or create your own.

Date: _____ Total days/hours of experience with preceptee: _____

Your preceptee's goals for the day: Be certain to describe behaviors that will indicate if goals are being met. How will you know the goals are achieved?

_____

_____

_____

_____

Notes on progress toward goals: Address what behaviors demonstrated progress and what behaviors need to be improved. Include a description of how you will plan for remediation if necessary.

_____

_____

_____

Preceptee goals for the next learning experience:

_____

_____

_____

Make a note as to what you need to do to facilitate your preceptee's next learning experiences:

_____

_____

FORM 1-2: PRECEPTEE REFLECTIVE JOURNAL

Use this form to track your progress. Share this with your preceptor daily.

Date: _____

Today's goals, which also include today's plans for improvement based on your previous experiences (be specific).

_____

_____

List any clinical activities that were new to you today. Also add any activities with which you have had minimal experience.

_____

_____

_____

Describe one of your therapeutic nursing interventions that required you to make a decision. Include in your description the dilemmas you encountered in your decision-making process. Describe the effectiveness of your decision, including all the possibilities that were considered. Share the rationale for your final decision.

_____

_____

_____

Reflecting upon today's goals and planning for tomorrow: Indicate if you achieved your goals. Describe ways in which you improved today. Describe behaviors that you want to work on next.

_____

_____

FORM 1-3: PRECEPTOR PROGRESS JOURNAL

Use this form to track your progress.

Date: _____

Today's goals, which also include today's plans for improvement based on your previous experiences (be specific).

_____

_____

List any encounters that were new to you today. Also add any encounters with your preceptee with which you have had minimal experience.

_____

_____

_____

Describe one situation with your preceptee that required you to make a decision. Include in your description the dilemmas you encountered in your decision-making process. Describe the effectiveness of your decision, including all the possibilities that were considered. Provide the rationale for your final decision.

_____

_____

_____

Reflecting upon today's goals and planning for tomorrow: Indicate if you achieved your goals. Describe ways in which you improved today. Describe behaviors that you want to work on next.

_____

_____

CHAPTER TWO

Considering Legal and Regulatory Controls

Action springs not from thought, but from a readiness for responsibility.

—Dietrich Bonhoeffer

INTRODUCTION

Before you get started with your preceptee, there are a few legal and regulatory controls you should consider. They shouldn't stop you or intimidate you. You should just check that everything is in place to ensure a good experience with your preceptee. The purpose of this chapter is to discuss those legal and regulatory factors that apply to you and your preceptee, including roles and responsibilities, orientation, liability, supervision, permissible technical procedures, health clearances, and contracts. As appropriate, the chapter points out different considerations for the new graduate and the student nurse. There are more references to student nurses in this chapter than in most of the other chapters.

OBJECTIVES

After completing the chapter and related learning activities, you should be able to

1. Describe availability of agency-specific documents outlining preceptor and preceptee roles and responsibilities.

2. Describe desired preceptor qualifications.

3. Identify (describe) possible personnel under whose supervision the preceptee may operate (if any).

4. Make arrangements for appropriate HIPAA and OSHA orientation (as needed) before starting the precepting experience.

5. Assess the status of the preceptee's license (fully licensed, interim permittee, student) as needed in the situation.

6. Describe the liability status of both the preceptor and the preceptee.

7. State the mandated technical procedures in the agency or school of nursing and those specific to the individual unit that limit preceptee participation because certification or direct supervision is required or the school of nursing does not permit it.

8. Describe documentation that requires preceptor cosignature.

9. Assess for any needed agreement or contract that might be required by the agency, school of nursing, or unit.

10. Describe preceptee required health clearance status.

QUESTIONS TO GUIDE YOUR LEARNING

1. Do you understand both your and your preceptee's roles and responsibilities?

2. Do you meet your state, agency, or school of nursing preceptor qualifications?

3. Must the preceptee always work directly under your supervision? Can you assign the preceptee to another registered nurse or staff member?

4. What orientation has been provided for the preceptee? What additional information is needed for orientation to the agency and to the particular unit in the agency?

5. Has the preceptee received HIPAA and OSHA orientation? If not, what arrangements for appropriate orientation are needed? How can you make it happen before you start with your preceptee?

6. Have you checked the status of your preceptee's license? Is the preceptee fully licensed, an interim permitee, or an unlicensed nursing student?

7. What is your liability as a preceptor during precepted experiences? What is your preceptee's liability?

8. Are there any technical procedures that the preceptee is not permitted to perform because certification is necessary or because the preceptee is a student and the school or agency doesn't allow students to perform these procedures?

9. May a student perform procedures requiring agency certification under your direct supervision? For those procedures requiring demonstrated competence, which can your preceptee perform?

10. Is there any documentation completed by the preceptee that requires your cosignature?

11. How will you determine the amount of direct supervision needed by the preceptee?

12. If you are working with a student, have you verified the student's liability insurance and any needed health clearances? Have you signed a contract with your student if the school of nursing requires this?

Roles and Responsibilities

Let's start with roles and responsibilities. Be sure you clearly understand your roles and responsibilities and that you are comfortable with them. Be sure to clarify anything you don't understand. The roles may be different for a new nurse employee than for the student preceptee. Those potential differences are briefly described. Also see Chapter 1 for further role descriptions.

Employee Preceptee

If you are working with an employee, your education department and/or your manager or supervisor should establish roles and agency objectives for precepted experiences. Others on the unit should also be aware of the precepted experiences. If your manager and other staff are not clear about roles and responsibilities, you may encounter problems that interfere with your preceptee's learning and progression. For example, other staff members may resent the "extra help" you are getting from your preceptee while you have the same number of patients as they have. Of course this is not reality. It takes more time, at least early in the experience, to work with the preceptee. Another problem might occur if you are assigned to a different unit or assignment periodically or if you are assigned to more patients than other staff.

Be sure you also collaborate with your preceptee to mutually establish clear understanding of both the role of the preceptee and of the preceptor. Depending on the preceptee, you may want to modify some of the roles and responsibilities. For example, if the student has been working as a certified nursing assistant or is a practical or vocational nurse returning for an associate or baccalaureate degree, you may want to explore the possibilities of what the preceptee is permitted to do; allow more self-direction earlier in the experience. Make sure others on the unit understand the rationale for this alteration in the usual preceptee progression.

Student Preceptee

If you are working with a nursing student, roles and responsibilities of the student, the faculty member, and the preceptor should be clearly spelled out in a written contract or agreement. Be sure you establish any limitations on the learning experience, such as technical skills the student may not perform. You should also be aware of the objectives for the student's learning experience as well as the student's personal goals.

Working with Other Personnel

You may want the preceptee to have an experience with another staff member or on another unit that works with the patients on your unit so that the preceptee experiences a continuum of patient care. Be sure to find out if placing the preceptee with someone other than you is permissible. It is particularly important to establish permission if your preceptee is a nursing student.

Preceptor Qualifications

It is very likely that you were selected to precept because you are knowledgeable and a very capable experienced employee whose mentoring and role modeling is expected to be exemplary. In many states, when working with a student a preceptor must be a registered nurse with at least 2 years experience in the agency. In baccalaureate-level programs, it is preferred or required (depending on the state) that the preceptor have a Bachelor's degree. In some rare cases this requirement may be waived. The state requirements, if any, should appear in the state's nurse practice act. In a draft position statement describing guidelines for preceptors in schools of nursing, the American Association of Colleges of Nursing (2007) stipulates that preceptors working with students, at a minimum, hold a baccalaureate degree in nursing. If you are working with a student, be sure the nursing program knows your degree and experience status. In addition, there are many desirable preceptor qualities other than your degree and experience. See Chapter 9 for more specific information on facilitative preceptor approaches.

Orientation

Orientation is critical to a good start in any job. A discussion about orientation is included in this chapter on legal and regulatory factors because it is an important part of responsible supervision.

Agency

Has your preceptee been oriented to your agency? If not, you need to make arrangements for this. The preceptee needs to learn about hospital policies and procedures. Most agencies have periodic scheduled orientations for new employees. It's likely your preceptee has attended one of these. You may want to introduce essential policies as they apply to current situations on your unit until the preceptee can attend a full orientation. If you are working with a nursing student, you may need to have the preceptee attend a regularly scheduled agency orientation before starting the precepting experience with you.

Unit

You need to orient your preceptee to your unit. A thorough orientation is very important for safe effective learning and supervision. It also gives you an opportunity to assess the capabilities of your preceptee. See Chapter 3 for a detailed description of a unit orientation.

OSHA and HIPAA

Your agency probably has an orientation to Occupational Safety and Health Administration (OSHA) and Health Insurance Portability and Accountability Act (HIPAA) requirements. Be sure your preceptee completes this orientation or make arrangements for these two orientations.

If you are working with a nursing student, your agency may have negotiated an agreement with the school of nursing to certify that the students have been oriented to the OSHA safety standards and to the HIPAA requirements. Check with the faculty liaison and the student to ensure all OSHA safety requirements have been met. The school of nursing should document (and maintain documentation) that the student has appropriate knowledge and skill for maintaining universal precautions, has had general and specific accident prevention instruction, and is cognizant of safety activities, fire safety, infection control, and universal precautions. You need to make the student aware of any related unit-specific safety considerations.

You may also need to explore whether the student needs agency-specific HIPAA orientation. You may want to ensure that your preceptee interprets the regulations for the use and disclosure of patient health information appropriately. You might ask what the preceptee would do in example situations both for OSHA and HIPAA to be sure the preceptee is ready to start.

You may want to look at the links below or have your student look at them for more information about these two important regulatory controls.

OSHA Links

- Comprehensive OSHA information from the U.S. Department of Labor, Occupational Health and Safety Administration: http://www.osha.gov
- OSHA laws, regulations, and interpretations from the U.S. Department of Labor, Occupational Health and Safety Administration: http://www.osha.gov/comp-links.html

HIPAA Links

- Comprehensive HIPAA information from the U.S. Department of Health and Human Services: http://www.hhs.gov/ocr/hipaa
- Summary of the HIPAA privacy rule from the U.S. Department of Health and Human Services: http://www.hhs.gov/ocr/privacysummary.pdf

Legal Considerations

There are yet a few more brief legal factors to attend to. Are you feeling nervous yet? No need. Doing a brief check on these areas should put your concerns to rest.

License Status

The agency has probably checked the license status of a new hire, but you may want to verify whether the license is permanent or interim and note the expiration date. If the preceptee is a student, of course there is no license, but you should be sure the student is registered with the university or college for the current session. This is legally mandatory.

Liability Status

When staff nurses work with students, they often discuss concerns about their personal professional liability when working with students and when working with new nurses. Your exposure to liability is not changed because you are precepting either a beginner or a student. Each of you is held accountable for behaviors expected of a person with a license or those of a student at a particular level in an education program. You are liable for adequate supervision and for appropriately assigning responsibilities and activities. You need to observe your preceptee to be certain that performance is at a safe effective level. You need to be sure the preceptee is able to safely perform the activities and procedures assigned or delegated. When you first start working with your preceptee, you should probably observe performance more thoroughly until you are comfortable with skill levels.

Ability to Perform Technical Procedures

Verify your preceptee's ability to perform technical procedures. Agencies usually have some verifiable procedures that require documentation of competency. In this case neither the beginning employee nor the student may perform these without the appropriate agency authorization. Check for any agency-required procedure competency documentation. Even though your preceptee is a graduate (a fully licensed nurse), your preceptee may not have performed a specific procedure or it may have been some time since it was last performed. You should discuss the degree of competence with the preceptee for those procedures to be performed in a shift. In addition, encourage your preceptee to let you know when your supervision would be advisable. It would be a mistake to have a negative relationship with the preceptee so that there was hesitance in seeking your help.

If your preceptee is a student, be sure you establish which technical skills the student is permitted to perform by the school of nursing. Many schools maintain a skills checklist or other verification of abilities to perform technical procedures. Obtain a copy of that checklist or other skill documentation. Also, check your agency policies regarding students. Some agencies do not want students performing selected procedures. Ask the school of nursing if there are procedures they do not want the students to perform. For example, some agencies or schools of nursing do not want students to do blood administration or venipuncture without direct supervision. For technical skills the student is permitted by the agency and the school of nursing to perform but is not checked off on a procedure, you should supervise the procedure. It is not advisable to have a new graduate or student perform a new procedure without your supervision.

Supervision

When you begin working with a preceptee you need to supervise activities quite closely to make an assessment of capabilities. After you have established abilities in commonly occurring events, you can (and should) allow your preceptee to carry them out without constant supervision unless there are unusual circumstances.

Remember, the new employees or students are held accountable for their actions; however, the student *must* practice under the supervision of the preceptor or another designated licensed nurse *at all times*. You may designate a substitute preceptor for special learning situations, but a student still is practicing under your supervision. *At no time* should a student be in the agency performing direct nursing care when you are not there to supervise the learning experiences. If you are ill or cannot work with the student for 1 or 2 days, you should instruct the preceptee not to come to the agency for those days. If for some reason you cannot be available for precepting for an extended period of time, another preceptor may cosign the student's contract with the faculty liaison and assume responsibility for your preceptee.

Documentation Cosignature

In some agencies nursing documentation must be cosigned for some procedures such as blood administration or wasting narcotics. Check the agency's cosigning policies for both a new employee and for a student. In most states only licensed personnel may take verbal or phone orders. Your student preceptee may only take such an order if you are also listening and cosign the order. Be sure both you and the preceptee know when cosigning is necessary.

Specific Nursing Student Considerations

A few additional legal considerations apply specifically to nursing students: liability insurance, a negotiated contract, health clearances, and workers' compensation. Establish that the student has current liability insurance and has completed health clearances (such as immunizations, physical examination, and tuberculosis skin testing) required by the agency and the school of nursing. It would be helpful if the student verified these factors in a portfolio to be given to you to ultimately be retained by your education department. While verifying these factors, it is the responsibility of the school of nursing, the faculty member, and the agency to ensure appropriate clearances. It is also suggested that you verify the information.

Liability Insurance

Many nursing programs require students to carry liability insurance. Although the nursing program faculty liaison should have checked the currency of the student's liability, it is also wise to verify the currency of the student's policy.

Contract

Most states and/or nursing programs require a written signed contract that is negotiated between both the school of nursing and between you, the preceptor, the faculty clinical liaison, and the student. The contract should spell out roles and responsibilities and the chain of command for communication among all constituents. Usually, agency contracts are established between administrative personnel before students are placed in the agency. See Appendix B for an example of an agency contract with a school of nursing. In addition, the student, the faculty clinical liaison, and you should sign a contract that spells out the student's learning objectives and responsibilities. See Appendix C for an example of the individual contract between you, the school of nursing, and the student. Lines of communication with the student, the faculty liaison, and the nursing faculty administrator in the educational institution should be clearly stated. If you have problems, you should contact the faculty liaison and/or the faculty administrator right away.

Health Clearances

Both your agency and the student's school of nursing have health requirements. Generally this includes a physical examination, several immunizations, and tuberculosis screening. Some states or programs may also require drug screening. Check to see that all health clearances have been documented.

Workers' Compensation

Each state has variations in workers' compensation. You should know the procedures in your agency should your preceptee be injured. Your agency has likely worked out established procedures should a student become injured while working in precepted experiences. Usually the school of nursing caries the insurance; therefore students are directed to the college or university for obtaining treatment and/or claims. Talk to your clinical faculty liaison to learn about the procedures if student injury occurs.

Preceptor Strategies

Working with the Beginning Nurse

There are four applications in this chapter to help you use the chapter information in your precepting experiences:

1. Make a checklist of things you want to be certain are completed. See **Form 2-1** at the end of this chapter for a sample tracking checklist that should help to remind you of everything you want to check. You may want to add any specifics that relate to your agency or unit.

2. Make a list of preceptee activities you want to supervise for the first week. Start with commonly occurring procedures on your unit.

3. Make a list of any concerns or questions you have. Discuss these with your supervisor or education department or with the clinical faculty liaison.

4. Use scenarios to help your preceptee apply OSHA and HIPAA requirements.

OSHA-Related Examples

•   If your patient was very confused and kept getting out of bed and wandering off, what would need to happen before using restraints on this patient?

•   If a Code Red occurred right now, what would you do first?

•   Your patient is quite obese and needs help in ambulation. What can you do to keep from hurting your back as you help her?

•   Mrs. Hubbard is on respiratory precautions. Where can you find the protocol for these precautions?

•   Using Universal Precautions, when should you wear gloves?

•   If you have an accident, such as sticking yourself with a needle after a patient injection, what should you do for your safety?

HIPAA-Related Examples

•   Mrs. Watkin's neighbor visits your patient. She asks you if they think they got all the cancer. How would HIPAA Title II guide your response to the neighbor's question?

•   Mrs. Watkin's son, who lives out of state, calls the nursing unit and asks you how his mother is doing. If you were following HIPAA Title II, what would you be able to tell her son?

Working with the Experienced Nurse

If your preceptee comes to your agency from another agency, most of the same considerations described about new nurses should be addressed. It is not necessary to sign a contract at your unit level. Any needed contract would likely be addressed by human resources in your agency. Most agencies would also have checked license status before you meet your preceptee. You would need to verify that agency-specific policies and regulations were addressed, such as uniform or dress requirements, HIPAA requirements, treatment procedures, unit policies, and immunization requirements. You might want to use **Form 2-1** at the end of this chapter to check off items that apply. Collaborate with your preceptee to identify familiarity with common procedures on your unit so you can plan appropriate skill progression. The rate of skill progression is likely to be different from new nurse and student nurse progression. Your preceptee is likely more able (and willing) to be self-directed in carrying out orientation activities and in becoming familiar with agency policies and procedures, but you should assess abilities before assuming readiness or before allowing your preceptee to exercise autonomy.

Summary

Hopefully you are ready to get started with your preceptee. You should have a signed contract before you start, and you should be clear about everyone's roles and responsibilities. You should verify a skills checklist, cardiopulmonary resuscitation certification, liability insurance, and a health clearance. Your preceptee should complete orientation to the agency and to OSHA and HIPAA policies. You are probably ready to plan an orientation (see Chapter 3). You should plan to supervise the preceptee quite closely at first to establish skills levels and accountability.

Reflection

- Refer to the section in the beginning of this chapter called Questions to Guide Your Learning. After completing this chapter see if you can answer the questions. Some suggested answers are included in Appendix A.

- If you are keeping a journal of your experiences, reflect about your feelings related to the responsibilities you assume when you precept another person.

- What concerns do you have about your responsibilities as a preceptor? What would be the best way to address these concerns? Who could you consult?

- Does everyone in the agency's organizational structure or lines of responsibility understand legal and regulatory controls as discussed? Who on your unit or in your agency would oversee these elements?

- If you have a student nurse preceptee, have you signed a contract? Are you familiar with its contents?

References

American Association of Colleges of Nursing. (August, 2007). *Draft position statement: AACN guidelines regarding faculty teaching in baccalaureate and graduate nursing programs.* Retrieved February 19, 2008, from http://www.aacn.nche.edu/Education/pdf/Facexpect.pdf

NOTES

FORM 2-1: TRACKING CHECKLIST

Preceptee Name _____

For each of the items listed, place a check in Yes, No, or NA (not applicable) that verifies the action has been completed or doesn't apply to the preceptee.

Yes	No	NA	Verified Completion of Item
			Valid license or interim permit with an appropriate expiration date
			Certifications
			Current CPR
			ACLS Certification (if appropriate)
			Telemetry Certified (if needed)
			Venipuncture certification (if needed)
			Other agency-required certifications (list each)
			Orientations
			Agency
			OSHA
			Injury Prevention
			Fire Safety
			Electrical Safety
			Patient Care Equipment Safety
			Hazardous Materials
			Radiation Safety
			Disaster Plan
			Security Procedures
			Restraints
			HIPAA Protection of Health Information Confidentiality
			Unit
			Code Blue Policies
			Infection Control Policies
			Universal Precautions Policies

FORM 2-1: TRACKING CHECKLIST (CONTINUED)

Yes	No	NA	Verified Completion of Item
			Immunizations or Titer and Health Clearance
			MMR, Polio, DPT, pertussis
			Hepatitis B
			Chicken pox
			PPD skin test or chest x-ray negative
			Health clearance verified
			Contract (if student)
			Contract signed by all parties, student, and faculty preceptor
			Roles of faculty, preceptor, and student clearly described
			Contact information for clinical faculty and school of nursing administrator supplied
			Preceptee holds current liability insurance
			Technical Procedures Allowed
			Completed agency required certifications (Please list and indicate if certified)
			Technical procedures requiring direct supervision each time (Please list)
			Cosignature Required
			List any documentation that requires preceptor cosignature

(continues)

FORM 2-1: TRACKING CHECKLIST (CONTINUED)

Yes	No	NA	Verified Completion of Item
			Miscellaneous Items to be Verified (list and check status)

CHAPTER THREE

Getting Off to a Good Start

Nothing great was ever achieved without enthusiasm.

—Ralph Waldo Emerson

INTRODUCTION

Now is the time to demonstrate great enthusiasm and commitment for your preceptor role as you begin the journey with your preceptee. First impressions frequently construct the foundation for relationship development. You will probably be working with someone who is equally enthusiastic and committed but may not be overly demonstrative because of feelings of role uncertainty. Use your social skills, your position within the unit, and your expert knowledge to ease challenges that your preceptee experiences while being integrated into your organization. Help your preceptee learn how things are done, the norms of your unit, and the members of the work team.

This chapter will assist you in organizing the initial experiences that will enhance your preceptee's entrée into professional practice. Comprehensive planning and enthusiastic implementation provide a solid foundation for a lasting relationship. So let's get started!

OBJECTIVES

After completing the chapter and related learning activities, you should be able to

1. Describe for your preceptee how your organization works by identifying organizational and unit values, power structure, and sources of nurse support.

2. Develop a plan for your preceptee's initial 2 to 3 days of experiences.

3. Describe a strategy for developing your preceptor–preceptee relationship.

4. Describe for your preceptee the routines commonly occurring on your unit.

5. Describe tasks, technical skills, and procedures that commonly occur on your unit.

6. Describe commonly occurring diagnoses, treatments, medications, laboratory tests, important documentation protocols, and unit procedures.

QUESTIONS TO GUIDE YOUR LEARNING

1. What are the values of your organization? How do you see them lived in your work? What one word would describe your organization? How does the organization enable or inhibit your ability to carry out your work each day? If you encounter problems, how do you deal with them?

2. What three things can you do to get your preceptor–preceptee relationship off to a good start? What steps will you take to optimize the chances that your preceptee is welcomed on your unit?

3. Recall your first days of working on your unit. What prominent memory of your first day of work do you have? How will you orient your preceptee to your unit? What are the four things that are most important for your preceptee to know about how your unit functions?

4. What knowledge, skills, procedures, and protocols will your preceptee need to know to manage the first 2 to 3 days of working with your unit team? Can you identify the team members who are integral to your preceptee's employment success?

5. What are the most common diagnoses, medications, treatments, common judgments or decisions, and routines on your unit that you know the preceptee will definitely encounter?

6. What strategies do you plan to facilitate your preceptee's progression? What do you need to know to help guide your preceptee's professional role development?

7. What will you do if your preceptee doesn't ask questions? How will you know if your preceptee understands all the information you are sharing with him or her?

Getting Off on the Right Foot

It is important to get off to a positive start. Having success in the first few days enhances your preceptee's ability to develop skills and knowledge throughout the precepted experience. Chances for a positive start are increased if your preceptee–preceptor relationship is transparent and is supported through an open trusting relationship. One of the most important challenges you will encounter as a preceptor is to develop a conscious planning process that allows the preceptee to maximize opportunities that enhance role development as a nurse. In this process you are also developing in your role as preceptor. In the beginning of the relationship, you are required to do most of the work in guaranteeing awareness about both aspects. As the relationship develops, more collegial collaboration becomes possible though it is important for the preceptor to maintain the leadership role.

The Organization

Organizations are made up of two or more people who are working toward a common goal. To facilitate work, structures are designed to define relationships, common goals, and performance expectations. These structures are commonly depicted in organizational charts that are diagrammatic definitions of the formal structure of the organization, that is, how it's supposed to be in theory. However, because organizations are staffed with people, the straight lines indicating authority and communication of the organizational chart become superimposed with complex mazes with many turns, dead ends, quick routes, and choices. This is the informal structure or the way things really are. To help your preceptee integrate into the organization, it is important to know the organization's functional reality as well as the theoretical plan for how things should be. Share your knowledge bout the mazes, the turns, and the quick routes and choices. Help your preceptee gain an understanding about how to achieve an outcome in the most expeditious yet ethical way.

Organizational culture varies from one organization to another and also from unit to unit. The culture defines the system of norms, beliefs, values, and assumptions that determine how people act, think, and feel about organizational situations (Schein, 1992). The culture may or may not reflect the written policies and formal reporting relationships. Organizational cultures evolve over time and are the framework that describes how employees behave. In getting started with your preceptee, describe the standards of behavior. An example might be found in how nurses communicate with physicians. Are physicians addressed by their first name or are they referred to as Dr. (last name)?

Knowing your organization's heroes and their related stories helps new nurses to understand the values and beliefs of its culture. For example, the hospital's annual Nurse Week celebration reflects the organization's values and beliefs about international nursing. The organization hosts an annual fundraising dinner. Proceeds buy medical equipment and supplies to support the hospital's "sister" dispensary in Tanzania. Each year the "Diane Smith, RN" story is told, describing how she began the hospital-to-hospital program and how she gathered the Tanzanian dispensary's first 10 stethoscopes, a microscope, and two-dozen twin bed sheets. Knowing stories such as these allows your preceptee to become an insider, to become one of the team.

Understanding the dynamic of play between organizational culture and the organization's power structures is important. Power is the ability to influence the behavior of others (Tomey, 2004). It may be derived from position, expertise, or respect. Power can be destructive or constructive. Where it is used constructively within the work environment, the values of mutual trust and respect and personal empowerment are evident. Take a minute to reflect on how you see individual and collective power demonstrated within your organization. What are the informal and formal sources of power and how are they structured? How do you use these sources of power constructively on your unit? How will you assist your preceptee in assessing and working with these power structures? You have assessed the organizational context in which your preceptee will be functioning. Sharing that information facilitates the preceptee's ability to work effectively within the organization. Now let's move on to the nuts and bolts of developing your plan for your first day's experiences with your preceptee.

The Initial Meeting

The two of you should have an initial meeting before starting your preceptor experience on a busy shift where you might have limited time for social interaction and for showing how things are done. It is essential to establish, clarify, and verify both your role as preceptor and your preceptee's roles and responsibilities. During this meeting, establish a plan for how you will work together. You may want to share some personal background information as a way to initially establish rapport. It is very important to develop an accepting, open, and genuine relationship. Expectations of your role as preceptor that facilitate relationship development are as follows:

- You must provide a safe blameless environment for your preceptee. Precepting requires patience and an open inquiring attitude.

- Educational opportunities abound in the workplace. Practicing new skills within the context of their application enhances learning. The preceptor relationship allows the beginner to internalize the role of nursing and to distinguish between textbook learning and the realities of professional nursing.

- You are a role model. Your preceptee observes and reflects on your professional behavior and performance. You must model and ensure adherence to standards of policy and procedure. A new nurse must have the opportunity to observe tasks and interactions before they are tried. Be attentive. Protect patients by promoting your preceptee's safe practice. Protect your preceptee from making errors in judgment that threaten patients, colleagues, or future practice.

- You must be knowledgeable and comfortable in providing care for the range of patient diagnoses occurring on your unit. Identify your preceptee's learning needs. Plan and implement the requisite activities to build skills necessary for effectively providing care for patients admitted to your unit.

- Provide a supportive environment that facilitates constructive feedback and mitigates problems encountered by your preceptee. Your role as a buffer for your preceptee is critical for success.

- Assist your preceptee in becoming a functioning member of the team. Ensure that your colleagues support your preceptee. Remember that you are not alone. Collaborate with management and educators to ensure that your preceptee has optimal learning experiences and is able to resolve issues of conflict.

- Practice active listening. Attend to what your preceptee says and how it is said. You will gain insight about your preceptee's level of comfort with the experience. Encourage open dialogue throughout the day's experiences.

At the initial meeting you may want to share work schedules and plan for the days you will work together for the first few weeks. Discuss essentials such as when the shift starts, when report begins, dress code, employee parking, and how to access employee lockers.

Collaborate with your preceptee when planning learning goals, objectives, acquired skills, and skills requiring additional development. Agree on how feedback will occur, share ways of contacting each other outside of work, and exchange your expectations for how the experience will progress.

It may take a shift or two before you can plan out the learning experiences; however, develop a progression plan early in the experience. For example, the first day may involve only observation or providing the care for one patient. On the second and subsequent days, additional experiences that are increasingly complex can be added.

Helping the Preceptee Fit in with the Work Group

It is important for the preceptee to fit in with the work group and to feel accepted by the unit team. Knowing about the organization and the unit culture helps. Sharing what you know about group norms, what people value, how they like to interact, how they work together, and anecdotes about idiosyncratic behavior gives your preceptee a jump start. Additionally, identifying team members and introducing your preceptee assist in work group immersion.

Progressing at the Rate of Your Preceptee's Abilities

Beginners may experience difficulty when working in a rapidly changing environment that is made up of complex situations. It is important not to overload your preceptee. Gradually add experiences and knowledge. Be certain that your preceptee can manage current situations before adding more complex tasks. Try to add responsibilities only as fast as your preceptee demonstrates requisite ability and willingness. Pressuring your preceptee to integrate knowledge and skill faster than abilities allow can stifle learning and possibly stall progress. Communicate frequently, assess preceptee readiness, validate your impressions with your preceptee, and then move on to more challenging learning opportunities. You can find a comprehensive discussion of this topic in Chapter 4.

Unit Basics

Identify for your preceptee experiences that commonly occur on your unit, such as patient diagnoses, treatments, diagnostic procedures, laboratory tests, work teams, technical skills, and unit routines. You will focus your preceptee's learning context and minimize the potential for preceptee overload by reducing the stimuli to which your preceptee must attend. Remember to start simple; progress only after you have validated your preceptee's competency with the experience, task, or skill; and add additional pieces of information as you go along.

People, Teams, and Collaborators

Make a list of the people within your agency and on your unit with whom your preceptee will be interacting. Use **Form 3-1** at the end of the chapter to list team members and collaborators. Clarify for your preceptee their roles, contact information, and effective ways of interacting with them. You may also add community collaborators located outside the hospital.

Describe nursing and physician chains of command. Design a case scenario and ask your preceptee to identify key constituents. Coach your preceptee by discussing the process for contacting each constituent. Role play the scenario, question your preceptee, and encourage rehearsal of responses to queries.

Identify for your preceptee commonly occurring medical services that are used on your unit. Introduce your preceptee to physicians and discuss physician communication techniques, the differing roles of the physicians, and how and when to make contact.

Commonly Occurring Technical Skills

Help your preceptee identify the technical skills that commonly occur on your unit. It would be important for the preceptee to master these skills to ensure effective nursing care. Audit your preceptee's technical skill repertoire and facilitate opportunities for your preceptee to practice needed skills. If your unit developed a skills checklist, you may want to use it with your preceptee. If your preceptee is a student, ask for a copy of the school's skills list. Review the list and enhance your preceptee's skill development through repetitive exposure to skills that have been used infrequently. Use **Form 3-2** to list commonly occurring technical skills.

Common Diagnoses, Treatments, Therapies, and Medications

What are the most commonly occurring diagnoses on your unit? What are frequently prescribed treatments and therapies? Are there common medication orders that correlate with the various diagnoses? Make a plan with your preceptee for learning about these diagnoses, treatment, therapies, and medications. Encourage your preceptee to read texts, articles, attend special classes, watch you, listen to you, and review the procedures manual. Help your preceptee list common diagnoses, treatments, and therapies by using **Forms 3-3, 3-4,** and **3-5**. Completing these forms provides a forum for discussion and review.

Unit Routines and Laboratory Tests

Understanding the unit routine helps your preceptee integrate into the work group with greater ease. Help your preceptee establish a routine by discussing what laboratory tests are ordered and when routine laboratory tests are drawn. Suggest that your preceptee review the most frequently ordered laboratory tests to validate understanding of why they are ordered. Discuss the significance of normal and abnormal findings and the related nursing implications and actions. Encourage your preceptee to use **Form 3-6** to help with beginning organizational skill development related to unit routines. Outline and discuss report practices, food tray distribution, time frames for assessments, staff responsibilities, the staffing structure, and communication patterns. Your preceptee will learn unit routines through observation of how you organize your work.

Common Decisions and Judgments

Core components of effective clinical judgments are evaluation, problem solving, and decision making. You can help your preceptee learn to think and make effective judgments as a result of experiences you set forth.

Evaluation

Data are gathered during patient assessments, from shift report, and from chart reviews. Discuss the findings with your preceptee. Thinking out loud enhances preceptee understanding of how you cognitively process facts. Help your preceptee make links between assessment findings to create a holistic perspective of the patient. Point out critical pieces of information and link the findings to your hypothesis as to what is happening with the patient. Quiz your preceptee by asking focusing questions that link small pieces of data with the pathophysiology associated with the diagnosis.

Diagnostic Reasoning

Problem solving occurs through diagnostic reasoning. Creating alternatives is evident in the more practiced professional. You problem solve based on your ability to generate various hypotheses. If your preceptee is a student or a beginning nurse, generating multiple hypotheses may be very difficult. Thinking out loud helps your preceptee understand how you cognitively process the facts into various solutions.

Decision Making

Decision making is a result of effective prioritization. As you gather data and make associations through reasoning, you arrive at a decision. Share your process of decision making with your preceptee. Encourage your preceptee to think out loud. Help develop effective judgment by guiding your preceptee's thoughts using questioning. Discuss your preceptee's rationale. Initially, it will seem like the process takes forever. Remember, it is your role to be patient and supportive. As your preceptee develops, the process will become increasingly streamlined.

For example, recall common or recurring decisions you make. If you are a cardiac nurse and your patient complains of chest pain, what do you do? If you're providing care to a fresh surgical patient who is complaining of pain, what do you do? How are the scenarios similar? How are they different? Discuss your thought processes with your preceptee. Explain how you arrive at decisions that require you to use your judgment as a professional nurse. What do you assess? What parameters guide your judgment? What actions do you take and why? Using real cases that you've experienced is a great strategy for creating the context in which judgments are made and decision making occurs. Remember, you are the expert; your preceptee is a beginner. Be prepared for questions for which you have long since forgotten the answers. You may use **Form 3-7** to assist you with describing your reasoning and decision processes.

Documentation and Communication

Effective communication is an essential skill for the professional nurse. Communication is not limited to oral skills but also includes skill development in writing and computing as most patient documentation systems are electronically based. To enhance your preceptee's communication skills you may want to do the following:

1. Invite your preceptee to observe you when you are speaking with patients, family members, and members of the care delivery team. Encourage actively listening while you're interviewing a patient, taking a history from a family member, or giving a report. Listen when the preceptee speaks with a patient, a team member, or on the phone with physicians. Offer suggestions that enhance your preceptee's communication skill development.

2. Gather forms, reports, and memos that are commonly used on your unit. Demonstrate the correct way of completing a form or report. Review your preceptee's report or form for accuracy upon completion, making certain requisite data are present.

3. More than likely, your preceptee will be required to attend a computer class offered by your hospital. Work with your preceptee to access electronic laboratory reports, pharmaceuticals, and so on. Demonstrate proper techniques for entering patient data. Anticipate that your preceptee will require additional time to learn the various programs. Review documentation standards and unit policies. One-on-one instruction is an effective strategy to enhance your preceptee's skill level. Finally, remember to arrange for a computer system password for your preceptee before the start of the experience.

Preceptor Strategies

This chapter included a number of strategies embedded with each topic that you may use with a student, beginning, or experienced nurse preceptee. There are strategic differences between the beginner/student and the experienced nurse.

Working with the Beginning Nurse

1. It is very common for a student or beginning nurse to attend to the varying stimuli found on a busy unit. Begin your experience by meeting with your preceptee at a location with few distractions, perhaps a coffee shop. Clarify roles and responsibilities. Collaboratively establish a plan for how you will work together. Exchange expectations, discuss how you will manage ongoing communication, and, of course, share contact information and work schedules. Also share unit essentials such as dress code, when the shift starts and ends, when report begins, and where employees park. Be open and enthusiastic in your communication.

2. Both the student and the new nurse preceptee share the role of a social outsider to your work group. It is important to bring your preceptee into the fold. Introduce your preceptee to coworkers. Review the formal organizational chart so your preceptee understands chain of command, the organizational system, and the formal power structure. Share your knowledge of how to get things done informally.

3. Use **Form 3-1** to identify team members and collaborators and discuss how to contact them.

4. Students and beginning nurses usually have limited experience with clinical skills. Your preceptee may give you a copy of the school's clinical skills checklist that indicates the technical skills required for graduation. Review the list with your preceptee to determine which skills require additional exposure and experience. Facilitate opportunities for your preceptee to gain experience with the identified skills. Use **Form 3-2** to list commonly occurring technical skills.

5. Assess your preceptee's level of skill progression. Identify learning needs and collaboratively create a plan for learning. Evaluate progress on a regular basis and reprioritize the plan as required. Allow your preceptee, with your guidance, to set the pace of learning. **Forms 3-3, 3-4,** and **3-5** will help you to identify commonly occurring diagnoses, treatments and therapies, and prescribed medications that focus your efforts.

6. There is a definite difference between your level of experience and the clinical experience of your student or beginning nurse preceptee. Help bridge the knowledge and skill chasm by thinking out loud as you create hypotheses in the course of decision making. Use coaching techniques to guide your preceptee's thinking. You can find more on this topic in Chapter 4.

7. Be certain you arrange for computer access before your preceptee's arrival to the unit.

8. Your preceptee may say, "There is so much to know." Such a statement is frequently paired with feelings of inadequacy due to minimal experience associated with the professional role. Give frequent feedback and praise, using specific details about the situation.

9. You are a teacher and a leader in your professional role. Model high professional standards because your student or new nurse preceptee will be observing your every move.

Working with the Experienced Nurse

1. Arrange for the initial meeting with your preceptee to take place in an environment without distractions. If you're meeting at work, find a place where the two of you can discuss goals and expectations of the experience without interruption. Agree on how you will work together.

2. If your preceptee is experienced yet is new to your unit, you may want to discuss commonly occurring skills and assess your preceptee's level of comfort when performing them. Even though your preceptee is experienced, some skills are idiosyncratic to your unit and your preceptee may have had little exposure to them. Seek opportunities that enhance your preceptee's skill development.

3. Ask your preceptee to share experience goals with you. Review commonly occurring routines, medications, procedures, unit policies, and laboratory tests. Identify for your preceptee the most frequent diagnoses treated on your unit. Assess your preceptee's level of practice and then revise the plan for goal achievement as necessary. Summarize the activities of each day so that experiences can be arranged to meet preceptee learning goals. Allow your preceptee to set the pace of learning.

4. It's important that your preceptee clearly understand the healthcare system's organization. Use organizational charts to illustrate the formal chain of command. Also describe the informal chain of command, identifying key coworkers who can assist in "getting things done." Share stories about your organization and its heroes.

5. Help your preceptee "fit in" by introducing physicians, allied health personnel, and administrators. If your preceptee worked with the same personnel in another role, clarify your preceptee's new role and corresponding responsibilities with your coworkers.

Summary

This chapter describes strategies for getting your preceptee off to a good start. It is important that your preceptee know how your organization is structured both formally and informally. When planning for your preceptee, it is recommended that you start with experiences that are simple in nature, adding complexity as the preceptorship progresses. Identify people, routines, medications, diagnoses, and laboratory values that commonly occur on your unit. Doing so helps to simplify your preceptee's entrée into the way things are done. Maintaining a supportive relationship encourages your preceptee to engage in open communication with you. Share your unit's orientation checklist. In its absence, use the Orientation Guide (**Form 3-8**) to focus your preceptee's first few days.

Reflection

- Refer to the section in the beginning of this chapter called Questions to Guide Your Learning. After completing this chapter, see if you can answer the questions. Some suggested answers are included in Appendix A.

- Is your preceptee a new employee? What do you think the preceptee should know about your organization's culture? How will knowing these things help in progression? What will you share with your preceptee about your unit culture to help him or her be accepted by the work group?

- As you consider strategies for getting your preceptee off to a good start, what do you believe are the most important things to include when planning for success? How will you incorporate them into learning experiences?

- Do you perceive that you and your preceptee are getting off to a good start? Are you giving feedback freely using supportive and enthusiastic communication?

- Are you making daily plans with your preceptee? Do you include your preceptee when planning for subsequent experiences? It is important to encourage your preceptee to identify needed learning experiences and to develop a habit of reflection and planning for improving performance.

- What will you do if your preceptee seems to be progressing more slowly than expected? How will you proceed with your preceptee to improve performance?

- Your preceptee is new to the community. How would you describe how your organization fits into the community? Is your organization a partner with the community?

- You're scheduled for a meeting with your preceptee at a coffee shop near the hospital. After introductions, you present your preceptee with a binder labeled "Preceptee Plan for Success." What will your preceptee find on the first page?

- Your preceptee is in report with you. You see her writing and erasing, writing and erasing. What will you do to facilitate her ability to gather appropriate information? What questions might you ask?

- It is your preceptee's first day on the unit. What tools can you share that will enhance organizational skills?

- You're explaining a patient's laboratory findings with your preceptee. You are thinking out loud and conclude that the physician will probably write an order to increase the potassium in the patient's intravenous fluid. You ask, "Do you understand why the doctor will order potassium?" You preceptee answers "yes" with a nod of the head. You're not convinced. What will you do to ensure that your preceptee understands the rationale for your hypothesis?

References

Schein, E. (1992). *Organizational culture and leadership.* San Francisco: Jossey-Bass.

Tomey, A. (2004). *Guide to nursing management and leadership.* St. Louis, MO: Mosby.

NOTES

FORM 3-1: INITIAL MEETING AND KEY PERSONNEL

Initial meeting: check off items as they are accomplished

❑ Uniform policies: dress code

❑ Discussed preceptor and preceptee roles

❑ Discussed goals and objectives

❑ Shared work schedules

❑ Discussed feedback loop

❑ Discussed time and location of report (include system of reporting)

❑ Shared contact information

❑ Shared personal and professional backgrounds

❑ Reviewed skills checklist

❑ Reviewed employee parking policy

Other pertinent information:

_____

_____

_____

_____

Key members of work group: List and describe preferences of unit staff, interdisciplinary hospital personnel, physicians, and community partners. Use this list to make appropriate introductions.

Unit Staff	Physicians

Interdisciplinary Hospital Personnel	Community Partners

FORM 3-2: TECHNICAL SKILLS

Think of commonly occurring technical skills and specific unit-based skills. List them and check them off as the preceptee demonstrates competency.

Completed	Technical Skills	Completed	Specific Unit-Based Skills
❑		❑	
❑		❑	
❑		❑	
❑		❑	
❑		❑	
❑		❑	
❑		❑	
❑		❑	
❑		❑	
❑		❑	
❑		❑	
❑		❑	
❑		❑	
❑		❑	
❑		❑	
❑		❑	
❑		❑	
❑		❑	
❑		❑	

FORM 3-3: COMMONLY OCCURRING TREATMENTS

List commonly occurring treatments, laboratory tests, procedures, and resources.

Treatments	Laboratory Tests

Procedures	Resources

FORM 3-4: COMMON DIAGNOSES AND SUPPORTIVE RESOURCES

List commonly occurring diagnoses and supportive organizational resources.

Diagnosis	Supportive Resources

FORM 3-5: COMMONLY ORDERED MEDICATIONS

Make a list of medications commonly administered on your unit. Encourage your preceptee to become familiar with them. It would also be helpful for you to share any unusual reactions or side effects that you have come to know in your experiences with administering these medications. Give this list to your preceptee and suggest that the unfamiliar medications be researched. Periodically assess your preceptee's knowledge of why the medications are ordered.

Medication	Potential Reactions or Side Effects

FORM 3-6: UNIT ROUTINES

List important unit routines and share them with your preceptee. Include special considerations that you believe are helpful. Examples: report practices, counting narcotics, laboratory draws.

Time	Unit Routine and Special Considerations

FORM 3-7: COMMON JUDGMENTS AND DECISIONS

Thinking about common decisions you make may be most challenging, yet it could be one of the most important sources of guidance that you share. Think of decisions you make—decisions that have become increasingly easier for you as you gained experience in your work setting. You can help your preceptee by sharing the templates of reasoning that you've created through your experiences. Think of common decisions you make and, over time, try to share them with your preceptee. Start by making a list that you later describe to your preceptee.

Judgment Decision	Key Points

FORM 3-8: ORIENTATION GUIDE

The student or beginning nurse (and some experienced nurses if your unit is very different from theirs) requires orientation to the unit. Use this guide to focus on everyday occurrences that one needs to know about and perform on you unit. This form can be used as a scavenger hunt so the preceptee discovers needed information, or you can go through it with the preceptee. When completed, use this as a tool to generate discussion. Add to this form as needed.

❑   How many patients can be accommodated on this unit?

❑   What is the staff mix? Include numbers of staff and titles or licenses.

❑   Where is report usually conducted? What is the procedure and how long does report last? If report is written, examine examples of report from the last shift.

❑   Describe the structure of this unit. Is there a charge nurse? To whom does the charge nurse report? To whom do you report?

❑   What is the nurse-to-patient ratio? Who supervises licensed vocational nurse (LVNs) and licensed practical nurses (LPNs)? Who supervises unlicensed assistive personnel?

❑   Who makes assignments for this shift? How are assignments made?

❑   How are patient care assignments structured? Why are assignments made the way they are?

❑   How is acuity determined on this unit?

❑   Review the patient care records. Are there nursing care plans or critical pathways for all of them? What information about intravenous lines is available on the record? Locate the patient diagnosis, date of admission, and age.

❑   What is the culture of the unit? Describe the attitude that staff members have toward each other. How do they act toward patients?

❑   Do you see any evidence of conflict on the unit? If so, describe it.

❑   What time are breakfast, lunch, and dinner? Where and when are patient trays delivered? Who passes the trays?

❑   Who is responsible for taking vital signs? What measures do "vital signs" include? Check vital sign documentation on two patients. Where is the documentation located? When should vital signs be concluded on your shift? Where are the blood pressure cuffs and thermometers located?

❑   It's time for breakfast. How do you verify the type of diet Mrs. Z should receive? Mrs. Z does not get what is ordered. What do you do? How do you order a different diet for her?

❑   Where are narcotics kept? Do you have a password that allows you access to narcotics? Find the area for documenting Demerol 100 mg. What inventory information needs to be documented? What is the procedure for wasting narcotics? Should wasting be documented before or after administration? Where does one document patient responses to pain medication?

FORM 3-8: ORIENTATION GUIDE (CONTINUED)

❑ Locate the medication administration record. How and where is a 0900 dose of oral medication documented? How is the site of an injectable documented?

❑ Find an empty patient room or unit. Turn on the television. Change the television station. Find the call bell. How does the bed work? Raise and lower the side rails. Raise and lower the head of the bed.

❑ Answer a patient's call light. Turn off the patient call light.

❑ Where are laboratory slips kept? Who usually completes the slips for a new order? When you obtain a specimen, how does it get to the laboratory? What is the procedure for STAT labs?

❑ Where is the crash cart? Who is responsible for checking the cart? How frequently is it checked?

❑ A patient's dressing needs to be changed. Where are commonly used dressings and materials stored? Where are extra dressings and sterile supplies located?

❑ Is there a central supply department? How do you obtain supplies not kept on the unit? Where is linen stored? Locate the blanket warmer.

❑ You need to contact a physician to report that a patient is vomiting. How do you make contact? Where is contact information located?

❑ You need to contact the pharmacy. What is the contact information? Where is the contact information for other supporting departments?

❑ Find the policy and procedure manuals. What is the policy for changing intravenous tubing? What is the policy for ensuring the safety of patient belongings?

❑ Find the job descriptions for LVNs and LPNs and unlicensed assistive personnel. What is the role of the LVN and LPN regarding intravenous therapy?

❑ The patient is incontinent of urine and feces. How do you document this in the patient record? When should intake and output be completed? Who is responsible for completing them and documenting the findings?

❑ Read the policies on documentation. Review a patient chart. Find the nursing admission assessment. Find one problem identified in the assessment. How is the problem documented to resolution or continued in the medical record?

❑ Your patient has a productive cough. Where should you document this?

❑ Where are most of your physical assessment findings documented?

❑ How are patient care problems resolved on the documentation sheet?

❑ Find the documentation on a patient's intravenous line. What solution is running? What size cannula is inserted? How much solution was infused during the last shift? When was the intravenous line started? How do you document partial fills on the patient record? Is the amount totaled with input and output or is it documented separately?

(continues)

FORM 3-8: ORIENTATION GUIDE (CONTINUED)

❑ The physician has ordered a new medication and two new treatments on your patient. Who transcribes the orders? Who is responsible for checking the orders? How are new orders communicated to the nurse and to the supporting departments?

❑ How is insulin administration recorded? Is it documented differently than other medications?

❑ Your patient needs a breathing treatment. Who does this? How are your ensured that it was completed? Who documents it on the patient record?

❑ Your patient is receiving heparin daily. Locate the last coagulation report. What is the difference between the control and the patient's clotting time? At what value do you report the findings to the physician? How is heparin administration recorded?

❑ What are the organizational philosophy and the mission statement of your unit? Of the organization?

❑ What is the policy for taking breaks? Who cares for your patients when you're off the unit?

CHAPTER FOUR

Working with Beginner Behaviors and Ways of Thinking

> I have but one lamp by which my feet are guided, and that is the lamp of experience.
>
> —Patrick Henry

INTRODUCTION

When you start precepting a new nurse (recent graduate) or a nursing student intern, you are working with someone who has had limited experiences with various realities of nursing. This new nurse is starting a very stressful transition into a very complex professional practice. You are in a position to smooth this transition, to recognize what the beginner is facing, and to be supportive as he or she begins to develop skills through constructive experiences. The purpose of this chapter is to describe typical behaviors the authors have observed while working with student nurses and in observing beginning nurses as they start their professional practice. Even when the preceptee is experienced, if your unit is very different the preceptee may behave as a beginner in some ways.

A beginner will perceive situations differently from you, will be unable to take in complex pieces of information as easily as you, or may be unable to reason and act in the same manner as you. To be more like you, the beginner needs to have access to knowledge and experiences you have gathered throughout your career. You developed your skills as a result of collecting many past experiences in similar situations and by developing meaning from your experiences. Realize also that the beginner comes to the experience with significant compassion for patients, has great motivation to practice ethically and competently, and has considerable anxiety about abilities to perform in the manner he or she has seen in other admired professional models. The acute care environment has become increasingly fast paced and complex and, to the beginner, presents seemingly impossible dilemmas that press against a desire to be competent. This chapter should help you understand beginners' ways of reasoning and behaving as well as their anxieties. It should also help you identify ways to support and facilitate the beginner's developing practice.

OBJECTIVES

After completing the chapter and related learning activities, you should be able to

1. Describe four factors that facilitate developing skill progression levels.
2. Describe commonly occurring beginner behaviors.
3. Describe five preceptor strategies designed to facilitate skill progression.

QUESTIONS TO GUIDE YOUR LEARNING

1. What four factors can facilitate skill progression?
2. What are three behaviors of a beginner (new nurse, student nurse intern)?
3. What are four ways to work with beginner behaviors to facilitate skill progression?
4. When a preceptee seems "frozen," that is, unable to make a decision or take action, what is one thing you could do to "unfreeze" him or her in the situation?
5. Beginners often ask many questions. What would be a helpful response to these questions?

Experience and Skill Progression

The beginner you will be working with has had limited exposure to the real world of nursing, has had limited practice with technical skills or has had no experience with some skills, and has almost no experience with the continuum of patients' responses to illness and therapies. These experiences are necessary for the development of a template for deciding what is wrong or right in a situation and for what should be done or not done in a patient situation. For example, after working with many post–intensive care open heart surgical patients, a nurse would generally be able to evaluate the situation of the next patient, see what's relevant in the situation, and make judgments that involve recognizing abnormal responses and knowing what responses resulted in positive outcomes the last few times when a patient presented similar phenomena. It would even seem as if the nurse in this situation acted automatically or intuitively (Benner, Tanner, & Chesla, 1996; Dreyfus & Dreyfus, 1986). Compared with the experienced nurse, the beginner, with little or no previous experience by which to judge a patient's response to illness or therapy, may *not* immediately know if the response was unusual or normal and would *not* immediately know what to do if the response was unusual.

Think back to your first experiences as a new nurse. Can you remember how you experienced events? Recall how experiences you collected over time, along with the support from others, created a template that guided your thinking and responses. As you have progressed professionally, you may now be unable to remember that process because your decisions seem to be automatic.

Experiences, along with knowledge, seem to be critical factors for progressing in skill development. The time required to develop advancing skills is influenced by four factors: the frequency of one's experiences, the stability of one's experiences, the feedback one gets about experiences, and the degree of engagement or involvement in experiences. Each of these factors is explained below. Keep them in mind as you apply them to facilitate your preceptee's progression.

Experience Frequency

With more frequent experiences, such as working full time on consecutive days or working more days per week, the new nurse or student collects similar experiences more quickly. These experiences build templates for understanding and acting when these or similar events occur again. For example, think about when you first started to drive. You could not talk or tune the radio, eat, or change the air conditioning settings while driving. You primarily concentrated on keeping the car in the middle of the lane. Judging speed on curves was particularly challenging. After months of practice, keeping the car in the lane and negotiating curves became more and more automatic. You could do these activities without thinking about them and could talk or concentrate on additional actions. If you only drove the car occasionally, getting to this stage would take longer than if you had driven almost daily. The same is true of the beginning nurse. Working full time rather than part time tends to help the beginner progress in skills more rapidly and consistently.

Experience Stability

The stability of experiences tend to facilitate skill development and progression. Using the driving analogy again, if you were practicing your driving skills in a different car every 2 or 3 days, changing from automatic to standard transmissions, your skills would progress more slowly than if you had the same number of experiences in the same car with the same transmission type. The beginning nurse should demonstrate skill progression more rapidly or steadily if experiences occur on the same shift, on the same unit, with the same preceptor. If the new nurse is moved to other shifts or other units, progression will occur at a slower rate. A common practice whereby the beginner is precepted a few weeks on the day shift and then placed on the night shift with totally new staff can considerably delay the beginner's skill progression. Decision making in experienced nurses is even delayed when they are placed on a different unit, such as moving from medical intensive care to surgical intensive care (L'Orange Etheridge, 1989).

Effective Feedback

Feedback that informs the beginner about the effectiveness, or lack of effectiveness, of both thinking and technical skills provides a source for experience, particularly when accompanied by reflection about the experiences. It is important to talk about experiences to establish awareness of what went well and ways to make an experience better when a similar situation occurs (Bandura, 1985).

Engagement and Involvement

Have you ever driven home from work taking the same route you've driven for years, thinking about an event that happened at work? Do you remember much about the drive itself? Can you describe events occurring around you during the drive? You're riding with a friend who is driving to a new restaurant in a new area of town. You're talking about a recent trip you took 2 weeks ago. You arrive at the restaurant. What could you describe about the route you took for the trip? If you had to drive back home, would you recall the way? If, instead of talking about your trip, you had been observing and thinking about the turns and the environment as you went along, you would probably be able to drive back. The same is true of the beginner learning from experiences by reflecting about experiences. Reflection helps to establish a rich memory and meaning from an experience. When a similar situation occurs again, part of the memories of the experience can be brought into the forefront of one's thinking and action. This reflection coupled with feedback from a trusted source helps the beginner collect templates of experience that includes both knowledge and performance skills (Benner et al., 1996).

Beginning Nurses' Behaviors

Based on the authors' experiences of many years working with nursing students and research involving nurses starting out in practice (Haffer, 1991), several beginner behaviors are described. These generalized behaviors occur primarily because of limited past experiences that would inform the beginner about what might be happening and possible ways of responding. As the beginner gains clinical experiences, reflects about them, and receives support from more experienced nurses, these behaviors should gradually disappear and be replaced by behaviors that are predictive of a more experienced professional nurse. It is our hope that you will use some of the strategies we suggest to support your preceptee in gaining and reflecting about experiences as you facilitate progression.

Depending on the preceptee's experiences in past clinical situations, the following describes typical beginners' behaviors:

- Establishing priorities may be challenging for one who has few past experiences in clinical situations. Beginners' past experiences have more often been related to completing required activities. Familiar routines tend to be a prominent focus of behavior. An important goal is completing actions in a planned order. Tasks, daily shift activities, ordered therapy, and charting required entries provide direction. For example, on one night shift a new nurse was assigned four patients, all in one four-bed room. One patient looked particularly ill. His color was not good, he was cyanotic, and he was lying still with his eyes closed. He was receiving an aminophylline drip and required a great deal of effort to breathe. Retractions and nasal flaring were evident. His nurse, a new graduate, had an established routine of assessing patients who were awake before going to report and then assessing patients who were asleep after report, allowing them time to sleep without interruption. She followed her routine on this night, not assessing the patient who was on the drip. When asked what she observed about the patient in bed 4, she said she hadn't noticed anything. She went on to explain that she allows patients to sleep a bit longer while she assesses those who are awake. Because of her limited experiences, she used her established routine instead of responding to the stimuli indicating patient distress. All participants observed in this study (Haffer, 1991) demonstrated similar attention to their routines. Having observed a participant for one shift, it was possible to predict how he or she would proceed in additional shifts. The same activities (routines) were completed in the same order each shift. As the beginner attains clinical experiences, it is important to facilitate the transition from focusing on established routines to establishing priorities based on patients' responses to illness and therapy.

- Planning goals for patients or planning for patients' progression may be challenging for the new nurse. Generally, the beginning nurse has limited experiences with similar patients. Planning for future events may be particularly problematic. One of the study participants described how she prioritized her activities: "I normally have certain priorities. The first thing I do is check my medications. The next thing I do is check my patients, which is what I started out doing this morning; looking at everybody, checking their IVs. The next thing I do is to deliver breakfast trays and then I have to do my classifications in the computer. If we don't have them in by nine, we get comments on our evaluations. Then I pass meds. It's pretty routine." Challenges in developing prioritizing skills result from the beginner's inability to anticipate the usual course of patients' illness and treatment and being unable to anticipate the amount of time needed to complete various activities. The beginner has not yet repeated tasks often enough to allow for anticipating needed time to complete tasks or seen enough patients responding to illnesses and treatments over time to anticipate responses or needed treatments. Helping your preceptee anticipate future events is beneficial to his or her progression.

- Today's complex healthcare environment is not conducive to getting everything done, which is one expectation beginners have for successful practice. One way of coping with the complexities of healthcare delivery is to focus on one task at a time. When observing study participants, beginners consistently made numerous trips from the nursing station to patients' rooms attending to only one task or procedure at a time. They did not combine tasks. They expressed concern that they would never be able to work faster or more efficiently and that they would always be running to keep up. Helping the preceptee see that attending to complex multistep processes, a step at a time, is necessary until he or she gains more experience and becomes more skilled in performing procedures. Helping the beginner reflect about and therefore see gains in performance efficiency should enhance the development of confidence and skill progression.

- Prioritizing assessments based on patients' responses to illness and therapy requires past experiences with similar circumstances so that the relative importance of assessments is perceived. Study participants tended to complete assessments according to their routines. Patients were most often assessed based on their room number; starting at lower numbers and progressing to higher numbers. That a patient's declining condition was described in report did not alter this order of assessing patients. Sometimes the last patient assessment occurred at 10:00 a.m. Based on your experience, helping the preceptee see what's most important and thus prioritize assessments helps to build this skill.

- The beginner takes in partial elements of a total situation, sometimes experiencing oversight of relevant elements. A simple example can be seen when one subject went into a patient's room to check on the solution in the intravenous (IV) bag. The IV was placed in the patient's forearm. The patient's hand was trembling. When asked what the nurse had thought about the hand, her reply was that she hadn't noticed it. She was focusing primarily on the IV solution bag and the IV controller. Seemingly not hearing or seeing some events; attending to only partial views of the patient status occurred during observations of all beginners (Haffer, 1991). Helping the preceptee become aware of what's important in situations facilitates progression.

- Beginners are strongly committed to being competent; at the same time, they have strong concerns that they may cause harm. Therefore when something unexpected or never previously experienced occurs, anxiety may interfere with the ability to think and make decisions (Benner et al., 1996). Beginners describe this as "freezing" (Raingruber & Haffer, 2001). When the unexpected occurs, beginners may remain disorganized for a period of time. Also, the beginner has great difficulty responding effectively to rapidly changing situations and may not be able to respond. The freezing behavior is very distressing to beginners. They share feelings of insecurity when they have experienced freezing. As an example, early in a shift a family member rapidly approached the new nurse saying she should come quickly because her mother was having trouble breathing. The nurse responded by quickly going into the patient's room, elevating the head of the bed, and then leaving the room. She then went to the laundry room and into the supply room but did not do anything productive in those rooms. Eventually, she conferred with the charge nurse, who advised her to return to the patient's room to complete a thorough assessment of the patient's condition. When later asked about her thinking, she described that she just didn't know what to do first, so she responded in an unproductive manner. She went on to describe that her level of anxiety caused her to stop thinking effectively. Once she received direction from another professional, she then was able to focus on what to do. She further described, "Once that happened, the rest of the day seemed to go bad. And sometimes it's real hard because I'm an RN. I have full responsibility. And yet, I still feel like a little kid as far as my own knowledge and experience is concerned. It's very frustrating. I've had times, even today, when I've questioned why I am in nursing." It is important to help your preceptee with ways to respond to freezing.

- Because beginners haven't yet developed a repertoire of commonly occurring patients' responses to illnesses and treatments, they regularly rely on the strategy of writing down pieces of information. The beginners in the study (Haffer, 1991) spent a great deal of time writing down ordered treatments at the beginning of a shift and writing observations throughout the shift. They kept clipboards with columns of things to do, checking off completed tasks as the shift progressed. On occasions when the clipboard was misplaced, the new nurse became momentarily stalled in the ability to operate. An example of using memory aids can be seen in one study participant's description of how she remembered everything: "I write down everything right away. What I do is on my clipboard, I make special columns—one is for abnormal and one for report. And so if I found anything abnormal, I wrote it on my clipboard so that would remind me. So that's how I keep track. Otherwise, I do forget if I don't write things down." As the beginner starts practice, support this behavior. Realize that it requires extra time. Eventually, with experience the beginner will be able to recall similar patterns of responses and will not need to write as many details.

- The beginner feels a strong sense of responsibility for his or her role but describes a lack of confidence in knowledge and skill to perform competently (Haffer & Raingruber, 1998). To ensure that actions and decisions are appropriate, the new nurse frequently asks questions and verifies decisions and actions by asking questions of more experienced staff. The study subjects (Haffer, 1991) asked from 7 to 21 questions a shift, most often of the charge nurse. Most frequently, questions were related to needing to know more about technical procedures and to deciding the meaning of symptoms. The complexity of patients' conditions and number of procedures the beginner has not yet experienced is substantial. Asking questions and verifying actions is essential for beginning practice. For example, a new nurse was asked what was involved in making a decision about a patient's response. She answered, "I didn't think I had enough knowledge or enough information to make that total decision, so I went to Louise to ask her advice." Another nurse described, "About the colostomy bag, I wasn't quite sure. I know I needed to let the gas out of there, but after that, I wasn't quite sure how to handle the situation. I went to ask how to change the bag." Many beginners described that they often believe they know the answer but ask a more experienced person to seek validation. Preceptors should note that beginners may feel uncomfortable asking questions. Support the beginner in his or her questioning. Questioning and validating helps beginners build confidence and competence.

- Because the beginner needs yet to experience patterns of patients' responses, possible explanations for unfolding events may be limited. The possibilities considered often reflect the practitioner's most frequent and recent experiences. The following is an example of one analysis of patient information. When deciding what was wrong with a patient a beginner described, "I asked him if he had circulation problems like if he had some kind of vascular disease. I mean I thought that was maybe what was causing the swelling." No other possible explanations for swollen ankles and feet occurred to the nurse. The beginner sees limited aspects of a situation and tends to close off looking for possibilities because he or she has limited experiences with previous exemplars. Helping this nurse consider other possible explanations for events facilitates advancing skills.

- See **Form 4-1** for a brief checklist of beginner behaviors.

Hints for Working with Beginner Behaviors

To help you facilitate your preceptee's skill progression, we offer the following hints to help you work with beginner behaviors:

- Remember that the beginner has limited experiences on which to base thinking and behavior. Depending on how much experience you have had and your level of skill, your way of perceiving reality and of dealing with it could be quite different from your preceptee's. Be supportive of beginners as they collect experiences. They learn much faster with supportive positive feedback.

- Encourage the beginner to ask questions. Make it clear that you expect questions. Assist the new nurse or student to think through to possible answers. Use guided questioning to help focus thoughts. You may want to ask, "What questions do you have about. . . . ? Where could you look for answers?" Or, "What information do you think you need?" This should encourage the beginner to generate questions and to seek information.

- Help with organization and time management. Encourage the beginner to discuss priorities with you and make suggestions for ways to increase efficiency. Increase the complexity of assignments over a gradual period of time so time management and prioritization skills can grow. You might want to start the shift by discussing the beginner's plans. Remember without much repetitive experience it is difficult to estimate the time required to complete a procedure. It is also challenging to anticipate variations in a patient's condition. You can provide needed information, help with anticipating future events, and encourage reflection about the situations. It is particularly helpful to describe details of your reasoning in this or similar situations. Discovering similarities between current and previous cases makes it more likely the beginner will recall events and apply learning in new situations with decreasing need for help from you.

- Keep in mind that the beginner may overlook things. Be sure to check with the preceptee frequently. Ask questions like "What will you want to look for?" and "When you . . . what should you look for?" Encourage reflection about things that should be observed or have been observed. Foster a habit of thinking about what has happened, reviewing what he or she was thinking, and generating possibilities for what may happen in the future or what might be done in the future.

- Keep the environment as stable as possible. Minimize distractions, and add new experiences slowly.

- Try to schedule for consecutive days of work.

- Often, when a person gets frozen (unable to think about what to do or to take rational action for a time), it is beneficial to focus on *one* thing for a moment, to deal with *one first step*, or to stop and plan what to do next. You might suggest to the beginner that if this happens to consult with you or go to a room where he or she can concentrate for a minute about what to do first. Sometimes if you suggest *one initial action*, the beginner will become unfrozen and continue with sound actions without additional prompting (Raingruber & Haffer, 2001).

- Help the beginner make meaning of all the pieces of information they have taken in. Help with anticipating possible future courses of patient responses and nursing actions. Remember, the beginner has had limited experience with patients' progress through illnesses. Help your beginner see what's normal and what's unusual. Share your past experiences as you assist the beginner. One way of helping is to describe for the beginner your thinking: what you are aware of in a situation, what stands out for you, and how you will (or did) proceed, including the rationale for your responses.

- Beginners try to sort out what they are seeing in reality compared with their theoretical learning as students. You can help them see that there are many individual variations in patients' responses to illness and therapy. You can also help your preceptee understand alterations in "by the book" responses by sharing your reasoning and by helping the preceptee think through possibilities.

- In rapidly changing patient situations, it is beneficial to help your preceptee complete some of the patient care tasks as events unfold while coaching his or her thinking about rationale for changes in the patient's condition and resulting responses. You may have the tendency to step in and take over in a situation to save time or for safety reasons. Try to refrain from completely taking over the care of the patient. If it does become necessary to take over, be sure to share your thinking and rationale for responses either as they are happening or after.

- Help the beginner generate possible causes or explanations for patient conditions. Ask questions that stimulate thinking about possibilities. Help validate hypotheses, finding ways of ruling them in or out. Help your preceptee discover answers whenever possible.

- If the beginner is doing one thing at a time in an unorganized manner, help with identifying ways to combine actions so activities become more productive.

- A process of reflection can help beginners organize their thinking. It develops meaning from experiences and makes experiences more memorable. Set aside time at the end of the shift to discuss the day's events. Encourage reflection about situations that happened during the shift. Help the preceptee identify what went well. Also assist in analyzing outcomes that were challenging. It may be helpful to ask the preceptee about what changes in behavior would have enhanced the situation.

- Talk out loud about your reasoning as situations are unfolding. Share stories about real-life situations in your experiences. Describe, in detail, what you were thinking, how you reacted to a situation, and reasoning you used in the situation. Details make the experience more real and memorable. Your preceptee will learn vicariously from your experiences.

Preceptor Strategies

Working with the Beginning Nurse

The following are typical beginner behaviors that you might encounter. Rehearse possible responses before they happen.

1. Sally has just come to ask you the sixth question and it's only 1 hour into the shift. What do you think about her decision-making ability? How might you respond to this behavior?

2. After report Sally stays in the report area taking notes for about 20 minutes so she can remember all she needs to get done. Do you know why this might happen? Would you want to modify this behavior or would you encourage it?

3. After taking lots of notes after report, Sally begins her routine, the same routine she follows every shift. Patients' needs are not the first thing the beginner attends to. How can you help the beginner focus on patient needs?

4. Rashid does assessments a little bit later in the shift than you are comfortable with. You would like more information about the patients earlier in the shift. What do you say to him?

5. You're used to taking care of five to seven patients. You want your preceptee to build up to this. How will you progress the beginner to this capacity?

6. Melissa has three patients. You have the other four. How will you know how Melissa is progressing? What are one or two ways you can keep track of her status?

7. Concepcion has started the shift fairly smoothly. She is working on her routines when someone comes up to her and says, "Quick, my father is coughing up blood." Concepcion goes to her patient's room. Several minutes after this happened you notice her going from one thing to another in the nursing station, not seeming to be focused on a task. What will you do?

Working with the Experienced Nurse

You are not working with a "real" beginner if your preceptee has had 3 or more years of experience. You wouldn't want to treat the experienced nurse the same as you would a beginning nurse. However, keep in mind that your unit could be quite different from the preceptee's previous experiences. In this case, the preceptee may operate more at the beginner level for some nursing activities. Assess your preceptee's skill level and use appropriate strategies. Even if the environment is quite different for the preceptee, progression will probably occur more rapidly than if the nurse was a practice beginner. As the preceptee progresses, you need to be sensitive to evidence of comfort and skill in varying situations.

Summary

This chapter describes beginner behaviors resulting from limited experiences in the clinical situation. You should have a clear understanding of the beginning or student nurse behaviors. Although you cannot infuse experience, you can help to make each experience meaningful and remembered in ways that facilitate progression. We described the beginner behaviors in detail and offered hints on working with beginners. Use the beginner checklist (**Form 4-1**) and the hints for working with beginners to assist you in finding ways of dealing with your preceptee's behaviors.

Reflection

- Refer to the section in the beginning of this chapter called Questions to Guide Your Learning. After completing this chapter, see if you can answer the questions. Some suggested answers are included in Appendix A.

- Four factors were described that facilitate skill progression: experience frequency, experience stability, effective feedback, and engagement and involvement. What specific plans do you, or others, have for optimizing these factors in your agency?

- What do you believe facilitated your skill progression as you moved from beginner to more advanced levels of professional practice?

- How many behaviors on the Beginner Behavior Checklist (**Form 4-1**) have you observed? For each behavior, think about how you responded to these behaviors. If unsatisfied with your response, what might you do in the future?

- As you consider the hints for working with beginners, what specific ways do you plan to apply these as you work with your preceptee?

- Discuss the Preceptee Reflective Journal (see Chapter 1, Form 1-2) at least every day or 2. Reflect on the experiences described in the journal soon after the experience and compare future similar situations if they occur.

- Your preceptee has difficulty prioritizing. How can you help?

- Describe three of your preceptee's behaviors that are troubling to you. Look at beginner behaviors and hints for working with beginners. What could you do to improve either your preceptee's behaviors or your feelings about them?

References

Bandura, A. (1985). *Social foundations of thought and action: A social cognitive theory.* Upper Saddle River, NJ: Prentice Hall.

Benner, P., Tanner, C., & Chesla, C. (1996). *Experience in nursing: Caring, clinical judgment, and ethics.* New York: Springer.

Dreyfus, H., & Dreyfus, S. (1986). *Mind over machine: The power of human intuition and expertise in the era of the computer.* New York: Free Press.

Haffer, A. (1991). Beginning nurses' diagnostic reasoning behaviors derived from observation and verbal protocol analysis. *Dissertation Abstracts International, 52,* 160B (UMI No. 91-17, 892).

Haffer, A., & Raingruber, B. (1998). Discovering confidence in clinical reasoning and critical thinking development in baccalaureate nursing students. *Journal of Nursing Education, 37,* 61–69.

L'Orange Etheridge, C. (1989). *An analysis of critical nurses' clinical decision making.* Unpublished doctoral dissertation, University of San Francisco, CA.

Raingruber, B., & Haffer, A. (2001). *Using your head to land on your feet: A beginning nurse's guide to critical thinking.* Philadelphia: F. A. Davis.

NOTES

FORM 4-1: BEGINNER BEHAVIOR CHECKLIST

Over a period of 2 to 3 days assess your preceptee's beginner behaviors. This should help you plan ways of working with your beginner.

_____ Follows a definite routine each shift.

_____ Follows planned routines rather than developing plans based on patients' states.

_____ All tasks seem to have the same importance. Has trouble deciding priorities.

_____ May often get behind in completing tasks. Has difficulty anticipating how long a procedure or task may take.

_____ When describing a patient's situation or state, provides few details.

_____ Tends to assess patients because this is a required activity rather than doing it for the purpose of gathering cues about patient's states.

_____ Completes assessments of patients according to the numerical order of room numbers rather than condition acuity.

_____ Misses patient cues (observations that could be made about assigned patients).

_____ Tends to deal with only one or two observations about patients rather than seeing the cues as interrelated.

_____ Gets disorganized or freezes when something unexpected occurs, particularly when it interrupts routines.

_____ Doesn't organize or combine activities so that several trips are made back and forth between patients' rooms and the nursing station, completing one task at a time.

_____ Takes copious notes during the shift to help in remembering things to do and things that were observed in patients.

_____ Asks many questions to verify ways of doing technical skills, decisions they need to make, and potential nursing actions.

_____ Usually thinks of only one possibility, sometimes two possibilities, that explain a patient's state or response to disease or treatment. Frequently acts on these possibilities without verifying them or shuts off thinking about other possibilities.

_____ Doesn't anticipate things happening in the future. Engages in limited thinking about what if some possibility happens or what else may be happening or explain what is happening.

CHAPTER FIVE

Helping with Time Management

Lost, yesterday, somewhere between sunrise and sunset, two golden hours, each set with sixty diamond minutes. No reward is offered, for they are gone forever.

—Horace Mann

INTRODUCTION

Much of nursing care has time-related requirements: treatments, medications, shift times (8, 10, or 12 hours), scheduled diagnostic procedures, scheduled procedures performed by other departments or personnel, documentation, and many other activities. In addition, with increasing patient acuities and staffing in short supply as well as increasingly complex therapies, it is crucial to use time efficiently. If working with beginning nurses (a new nurse or student nurse) you will note they have significant problems with time management. You might even find yourself wondering what your preceptee is doing and why it's taking so long.

Compounding beginner problems are the classic time consumers (Williams, n.d.) that affect all of us. Commonly occurring time wasters include events that can't be anticipated or controlled such as telephone interruptions, visitors, socializing with others on the team, or doctors arriving unpredictably, needing help with some activities. Other factors include personal characteristics such as not delegating when appropriate, trying to do too much at one time, or procrastinating (such as putting off changing an ugly complex dressing or calling a doctor who typically gets angry).

This chapter is designed to help you understand time management problems your preceptee is likely to have and to be a guide for ways to help your preceptee gradually develop time management skills. If your preceptee is an experienced nurse but new to your agency or unit, it may be necessary to help with time management initially. However, you might anticipate that with experience, time management skills should progress much more rapidly than when the preceptee is just beginning practice.

OBJECTIVES

After completing the chapter and related learning activities, you should be able to

1. Identify (list) personal time wasters.
2. Identify (list) personal strategies for effectively managing your time.
3. Collaborate with your preceptee to identify (describe and list) time management challenges and develop (practice) strategies for decreasing identified problems.
4. Describe preceptee's progressive time management improvements.

QUESTIONS TO GUIDE YOUR LEARNING

1. What are your own time wasters?
2. What are some time management strategies you use? How can you share these with your preceptee?
3. How do you prioritize your activities at the beginning of the shift? Have you shared this with your preceptee?
4. What time management problems have you observed in your preceptee, both beginner and classic problems?
5. What one strategy can you use to reduce two beginner time management problems?
6. What problems do new nurses or student nurses have with delegating?
7. What are two strategies you can use to refine your preceptee's classic time management problems in each of the areas below:
   a. Organizing and prioritizing
   b. Delegating
8. What strategies for improving time management can you use when precepting a more experienced nurse?

Time Management Issues

Let's first look briefly at the time management issues you are likely to encounter. They include beginner behavior problems and classical internal and external time management problems. It is important to identify both your own and your preceptee's time management practices and problems. You can then share what works for you and target your preceptee's time stealers so you can help gradually improve his or her use of time.

Assessing Time Management Practices

How can you help your preceptee develop efficient time management skills? You can provide many models of effective time management, many of which your preceptee may adopt in his or her behaviors. However, you need to include some deliberate activities to help your preceptee deal with beginner problems and decrease time wasters. First, you may want to assess your own ability to manage time wasters to model effective time management for your preceptee. Then, in this section several strategies are offered for identified time management problems.

Assessing Your Time Management

If you are quite experienced and confident in your time management skills, you may want to skip this; however, your management activities may be quite automatic so that it is difficult to share your strategies (make them visible) with your preceptee. Try the following strategy to discover how your time is used and how you act to reduce time wasters: Using **Form 5-1**, jot down what you're doing every 15 minutes for 2 hours during your work day. Be accurate with your description so you can analyze your time wasters. Write about your observations frequently while they are clear in your memory. If you wait until lunch break or the end of shift, you may forget about some events and perhaps miss some time waster patterns.

How effective are your time management skills? If you tend to perform activities that are unplanned, how can you plan for them in the future? Do the unplanned activities need to be integrated into your work load or do you need to brush up on your delegation skills? Do you have a clustering of unplanned activities that fit those identified in the "internal time wasters" list? What can you do differently to minimize the unplanned activities?

Assessing Your Preceptee's Time Management

Polished, efficient, time management skills are not likely unless your preceptee is an experienced nurse. Before developing strategies to assist your preceptee in improving time management behaviors, it may be helpful to collaborate with your preceptee in analyzing current management skills and time wasters. You may first want to discuss how the preceptee usually organizes activities and how activities are prioritized. **Form 5-1** can also be used by the preceptee to generate an awareness of how time is spent and how it is wasted.

Taking Action to Effectively Manage Time

The assessment activities above should help you target your preceptee's most frequent or significant time management problems first. If your preceptee is an experienced nurse, your goal for the precepted experience might be efficient and effective time management skills, which is probably realistic. If your preceptee is a beginner (a new nurse or student nurse), the same goal is not realistic. Progressive improvement occurring over time is more likely. For the beginner, performance will develop very gradually, as reflection to improve performance and practice experience occurs. It takes time to accumulate enough experience to become effective and efficient. In this section, typical time management problems are described as well as strategies to address them.

Beginner Time Management Problems

Largely due to a lack of experience, beginners have to grapple with a long list of problems that use their time and interfere with effective time management:

- Performing procedures slowly.
- Focusing on routines rather than on factors that guide prioritizing such as patient responses to illness and therapy.
- Limited ability to anticipate patient responses to illness or therapy and other future events that are likely to happen.
- Inaccurately judging time required to complete procedures.
- Starting the shift with a plan but failing to quickly reorganize when any interruption of routines occurs.
- Taking time to write lots of notes.
- Performing activities one at a time rather than combining activities.
- Needing time to ask questions.
- Delaying some activities (procrastinating).
- Being unsure of ability to delegate.

These behaviors "steal" valuable time. Beginners believe they are working as fast as they can and that they will never improve their ability to remain on task. Believing this is very discouraging and may affect job satisfaction and prompt changes in career settings.

Classic Time Management Problems

When describing time management problems, most often the topic of time wasters is the focus. Ahmad (2007) described time wasters in two categories, internal and external time wasters. Internal time wasters involve things within the individual that waste time, things *controlled by you* that waste time. External time wasters are not as easy to control. As the term suggests, these are events *outside of your influence* that waste or use your time.

Internal Time Wasters

Examples of internal time wasters include the following:

- Procrastination: Delaying calling a doctor who can be crabby or delaying a complex procedure.
- Disorganization (poor planning or prioritization): Going back and forth to the nursing station, misplacing notes and spending time looking for them, completing routine activities without considering priorities so that unplanned events begin to interfere with organization.
- Failure to establish goals: Using only established routines for goals rather than patients' responses to their illnesses and treatments as a basis for goals or ways of organizing.

- Management by crisis: This results from disorganization and poor planning. Responding to problems as they crop up because they were not anticipated, leading to delay of planned or scheduled activities.

- Inability to delegate: Performing activities that a licensed vocational nurse or aide or unit assistant could do; being unsure of authority to delegate.

- Inability to say "no": When asked to do something to help a coworker, agreeing to help although already behind rather than saying "no."

- Haste or ineffective behavior: Frequently, the faster the beginner works, the more behind he or she gets because, in haste, things are forgotten or they are not done right so they have to be repeated or fixed.

- Indecisiveness: Having difficulties deciding what to do first or next; being unsure of what to do and/or who to ask.

- Lack of relevant skills: A procedure that has been forgotten or never previously performed or the procedure has changed and knowledge is lacking.

External Time Wasters

These are events that are unpredictable or unscheduled and not easily controlled. They are under the control of others. They take time away from planned, previously prioritized, and organized activities. Below are some examples of these types of time takers that may be experienced either by you or your preceptee.

- Visitors/families: Families and visitors have questions or concerns about something and want you to stop what you are doing so you can talk with them.

- Telephone calls: Families or doctors can call just as you have another crisis occurring.

- Coordinating activities with other departments: You are waiting to discharge someone, taking a patient to another service, or need a preoperative medication that isn't yet on the unit.

- Lack of information: You don't know how to do something, or there has been a failure in communication (such as omissions of patient changes in report). You have to spend unplanned time to gather information. Perhaps you have to contact a physician to get needed information, which requires several attempted calls.

- Socializing: Your team culture may be one where there is a great deal of socializing among the group members.

Preceptor Strategies

Working with the Beginning Nurse

Depending on your preceptee's nursing experiences the behaviors described about beginner time management problems will occur to some extent. So what can you do to reduce beginner time thieves? The following are suggestions for you to try:

1. Share some of your time management strategies with your preceptee. Describe them and why you find them useful.

2. Be positive in your responses and suggested behavior changes. Remember the beginner already feels a lack of confidence, so work on being patient. Tell the preceptee what to do rather than what *not* to do.

3. Encourage questions. Also encourage your preceptee to attempt answers or discover ways of finding out answers when there is time and you believe the preceptee can answer.

4. Start the shift spending some time helping the preceptee plan and organize shift activities. Help the preceptee anticipate future events. You may want to encourage the preceptee to develop a worksheet or use an already developed worksheet that is specific to your unit. See a sample of a basic worksheet in **Form 5-2.**   A resource for other worksheets is *Nursing Worksheets* (http://www.minnesotanurse.com/work_sheets.htm). Describe for the preceptee elements that would be most helpful on a worksheet such as diagnosis, treatments, doctor's name, diet (particularly special diets or nothing by mouth), diagnostic tests, and surgery, including date of surgery.

5. If your agency supplies personal digital assistants (PDAs) or other portable electronic devices, encourage their use to facilitate the preceptee's time management. PDAs afford access to extensive resource materials, including organizational and time management tools. Software is available for drug databases, laboratory test data, medical calculators, and guidelines for care plans among other tools. PDAs may assist with documentation, medication and treatment scheduling, assessment data, and report information, which may free the nurse for other activities or eliminate duplicated effort. Davenport (n.d.) and Chang and Lutes (n.d.) provide extensive helpful information on PDA possibilities.

6. Anticipate procedures for which the preceptee may need review or help.

7. Help the preceptee anticipate events that may be problematic and with planning for potential responses.

8. Encourage the preceptee to tell you right away when starting to fall behind or needing your help rather than continuing in a struggle to catch up.

9. Consult with the preceptee frequently. Assess if help is needed with planning or reorganizing.

10. If unexpected events occur, help the preceptee reorganize.

11. If some emergent situation occurs, work alongside the preceptee to get things back on track. Use your judgment about the needed help. Try not to help any more than necessary and yet maintain patient safety.

12. If your preceptee puts off some troublesome activities (procrastinates), help with plans for ways of addressing the problem. For example, if calling a grumpy doctor is feared, work with the preceptee to rehearse what might be said. If the challenge is completing a complex procedure, review the procedure or talk the preceptee through

the procedure. Work with the preceptee (if necessary) rather than insisting it be done alone.

13. You may want to use **Form 5-3** to track your preceptee's improvement. It may help the preceptee to see that improvement is occurring. Helping your preceptee deal with beginner problems should enhance job satisfaction and help in retention. It may be useful to look back at tips for working with beginners in Chapter 4.

14. Encourage reflection about events of the shift. Plan to spend some time after the shift to discuss activities that went well and to identify strategies for improvements. Pay particular attention to comparing similar past events that should help the beginner with recall the next time something similar happens. You may want to do this away from the unit to avoid interruptions.

Preceptor Strategies for Reducing Internal Time Wasters

To help reduce internal time wasters, focus on helping your preceptee prioritize and organize to meet priorities, identify appropriate delegation opportunities, gain experience and confidence in skills, and reduce indecisiveness.

Organizing and Prioritizing

Many of the internal time wasters are related to problems with organizing and prioritizing. The ability to prioritize and reprioritize as events dictate changes is crucial to effective time management (Waterworth, 2003). Nurses new to your agency, even more experienced nurses, need your help developing priorities and organizing time when beginning to work on your unit. It is important to help the new employee with organizing for the customs of your particular unit in addition to the agency policies and procedures. You can also be helpful by sharing your experiences about the commonly occurring diagnoses and treatments on your unit. You can help the new person anticipate events in the future and with reorganizing when changes in patients emerge during the shift.

As described under the strategies for beginners, the new nurse or student nurse needs considerable help with prioritizing and organizing. Ask the preceptee about plans for the first hour or 2 at the beginning of the shift and periodically during the shift. Ask how your preceptee prioritizes activities and plans to accomplish first. To help with time organization, you might consider assisting your preceptee to develop an effective worksheet. **Form 5-2** provides a sample worksheet. During the shift, offer suggestions about the preceptee's process of prioritization. Give your preceptee feedback throughout the shift. Be positive and specific with your critical analysis. A comment such as "You're not being very successful at time management today" is not as effective as giving specific suggestions regarding strategies that increase time management effectiveness. "How about giving the insulin to Mrs. Bright before you discharge Mr. Moody. That might enhance your use of time," is far more helpful than the casual observation that your preceptee is failing in time management strategies.

Sometimes a preceptee will not assign enough time to complete a task. With experience, the preceptee can predict how much time commonly recurring tasks require, particularly if you periodically reflect with the preceptee about the time tasks have taken. Also, help the preceptee identify potential unplanned activities that might emerge as a result of a patient's condition. For example, the hemoglobin and hematocrit values are decreasing on a second-day postsurgery patient. The patient has two units of blood typed and cross-matched. You might prompt the preceptee to discuss his or her perception of how the two variables are related. You might need to suggest the possibility that blood might be administered during your shift. You might also review the policies and procedures for that activity.

Delegating and Saying "No"

In one study examining how nurses use their time (Lacey & Shaver, 2002), findings describe that nurses spend an average of 43% of their time on direct patient care, with the remaining time spent on documentation, supervision, and management of staff. In another study (Gran-Moravec & Hughes, 2005), findings describe that registered nurses spend 39% of their time performing activities that only registered nurses can perform. They also reported that 12% of the nurse's time involved performing activities that certified nursing assistants could perform alone and 49% of their time on tasks that both registered nurses and certified nursing assistants must perform together.

Frequently, there is too much work to be accomplished by one person. Sharing that work is accomplished through delegation, getting work done through others. Delegation is a learned skill and is integral to effective time management. If your preceptee has little experience in delegation, it is important that you provide guidance in learning to delegate appropriately and effectively.

Believing that delegation equates with a lack of ability to complete a job, your preceptee may not delegate. In addition, the preceptee might feel better equipped to complete the task and may want to do the "whole job" independently. Frequently, this response is related to a lack of trust in ancillary staff capabilities. The preceptee, new to the environment, may not know who to trust. Finally, your preceptee might feel uncomfortable delegating work because of a belief that the ancillary staff may not "like" that. Your preceptee may use under-delegation as a strategy to integrate with the staff.

Sometimes preceptees delegate inappropriately, such as delegating a task that the delegate is neither supposed to perform nor is capable of performing. It is advisable to discuss and model appropriate delegation strategies for your preceptee. You may want to discuss these points with your preceptee (American Nurses Association and the National Council of State Boards of Nursing, 2007; Hudspeth, 2007; Pierce, 2006). Briefly, these strategies include the following:

1. Assuming responsibility for patients' care regardless of what is delegated. The nurse can delegate components of care but not all of the nursing process.

2. Deciding to delegate involves judgments about patient's responses to illness and treatment, agency policies about permissible procedures and care, assistant capabilities, delegate's competence, and state law.

3. Assessing delegate for appropriate knowledge and skills to perform tasks.

4. Communicating specific, clear, complete, and accurate directions to the delegate and verifying understanding.

5. Following the delegation rights: right task, circumstances, person, directions, communication, supervision, and evaluation.

6. Assessing and evaluating delegate performance, and providing feedback to the delegate.

It is important to work with your preceptee to help with appropriate delegation. As a part of discussing priorities and planning activities, question your preceptee about delegation possibilities. During the shift you might explore delegation opportunities with your preceptee. Whenever the preceptee's time management is faltering or at the end of the shift, engage in reflection with the preceptee about what could have been delegated as well as what was delegated effectively.

Also be sure to support your preceptee in learning to say "no" in a diplomatic way such as negotiating either an alternative way of helping or an alternative time. For example "I can help you in about a half hour."

Gaining Skills

Gaining skills applies particularly to the beginner but also to a more experienced nurse if there has been no experience on a unit like yours. As the preceptor, it is important to determine basic skills in which your preceptee has acquired competency. It is also important to be sure your preceptee has experiences with commonly occurring technical procedures on your unit. List these procedures on a checklist. Plan for experiences that help to develop competence in the identified skills. Be sure the preceptee also takes responsibility for identifying opportunities to practice these skills. Begin with simpler or less complex procedures and then move to more complex procedures. Add experiences gradually so that the preceptee doesn't become overwhelmed. It is important to build confidence in skills rather than just adding experiences.

Before you have your preceptee perform a new skill, verbally review the process. Support the preceptee as necessary in performing the skill. If it is very complex, you may want to model the procedure before the preceptee does it. Use positive communication with language that conveys what should be done. Reinforce activities that were done well. Avoid criticizing with comments like, "Well that didn't go well" or " My, you're all thumbs." A different response that is more likely to help the learner know what improvement would make performance even better might be "That procedure went quite well." "Next time you could try to visually identify the meatus, before you clean the labia." You might also encourage self-direction by asking, "What did you think of that experience?" "Is there anything you would do differently next time?"

Dealing with Indecisiveness

If your preceptee is a new nurse or a student, you will probably see a lack of confidence in making decisions. Beginners frequently seek validation for the decisions they make. They want to make sure their decision was the right one to make. Also, when they are unable to make a decision, they seek advice from team members whose judgments they respect. Depending on the situation, it would be helpful to encourage the preceptee to make the decision rather than you making it. If the preceptee has no clue about an appropriate answer, then helping to think it through by guiding the thinking process should help to build confidence and skill. It is also useful to the beginner to hear about how you make decisions. When something occurs on the unit that involved your decision making, share the process with your preceptee. Beginners have told us that hearing these "stories" is like walking in the shoes of the story teller, an experience they can add to their repertoire.

Preceptor Strategies for Reducing External Time Wasters

Work with your preceptee to find ways to deal with these unpredictable events. Share responses you have found that decrease the interruptions or consequences caused by the time thieves.

First, help the preceptee find ways to reprioritize when these types of time wasters occur. Help the preceptee identify the activities that must be done first, followed by those activities that need to be done but that can wait, those that can be delegated, and those that can be left for the next shift or tomorrow. It is not uncommon for the beginning nurse or student to become so focused on one task that awareness of time and other priorities is lost, which leads to getting quite behind in achieving priority activities. Be sure to assess progress frequently during the shift, and help the preceptee refocus and reorganize.

Other staff can be relied on to help when time demands become overwhelming, but be sure to advise the preceptee to do this sparingly. When team members take over some duties of the person who is behind, it can interfere with the team members' time management. One common complaint about new nurses is that they spend too much time with one or two patients (failing to prioritize), which causes them to fall behind in meeting time lines. When the preceptee has to ask for help too often, staff members that fill in can become resentful.

Help the preceptee develop skills in dealing with visitors, family, and patients. Assist with developing abilities to manage how time is spent rather than having others "manipulate" the time. This can be viewed as a kind of time trading or shifting. Finding ways of maintaining one's own priorities without ignoring other time demands is an important strategy for a new nurse to learn. As a preceptor it would be helpful to provide some examples of time shifting when responding to common interruptions:

1. When making a quick initial round on patients at the beginning of the shift, describe ways of avoiding spending a long time with any one patient who wants to have an extended conversation. To avoid this rather than asking the patient how he is doing, it might be more efficient to initially tell the patient you are just taking a quick peek at all your patients and that you will be back later unless he needs something right now, or suggest that he call if he needs something before you get back.

2. A family rushes up to you wanting to talk about the plan of care for their mother. You are responding to a patient's alarming IV. Rather than talking to the family at that moment, you could suggest you will come back in a few minutes to talk to them as soon as the IV is checked.

3. It helps to break tasks into parts of the total task. For example when the IV was alarming, because of infiltration, you could first turn off the IV, then go back to the

family, tell them you need to restart an IV, and that you will return to talk to them. You could, instead, turn off the IV and discontinue it, then later return to start a new IV, and in the meantime go back to the family and talk to them. Alternatively, you could delegate the task to another nurse and then later help that nurse with another task.

In each of these examples you are trading or shifting how you spend time in a way that is efficient and that meets both your needs and others' needs.

Another problem in managing time is either rearranging your time to meet another department's demands or waiting for other departments or personnel to complete a required activity. Significant time can be lost while waiting for a medication from the pharmacy or for the laboratory to draw blood. Although these events affect time management, they are not under your direct control. What is in your control is resetting priorities and reorganizing. Help your preceptee alter priorities and organize so time wasting, while waiting, is minimized.

Working with the Experienced Nurse

If you are precepting a new employee who has had 3 or more years of nursing experience, you need to assess time management skills and help with orienting to the time factors specific to your unit. It is important to orient the preceptee to the routines that are time based on your unit, typical time management problems, departments with which you need to collaborate, and any team approaches used on your unit that involve time management. After the initial weeks of working with the new employee, you probably won't need to check your preceptee's priorities and time management skills as frequently. It would be a mistake to be too directive, but be sure to let the preceptee know you are eager to help as needed.

If your unit is very different from the preceptee's prior experiences, such as moving from a critical care unit to a medical-surgical unit, the preceptee may need coaching for a longer period of time. The skills sets in these two units are very different. Your preceptee will need to learn how to manage more than one or two patients. Learning to prioritize, organize, and reprioritize takes time and your guidance.

Summary of Preceptor Strategies for Developing Sound Time Management

Many strategies have been described for the beginner problems, classic problems, and for working with the experienced nurse. The following is a brief summary of preceptor roles for helping your preceptee develop effective time management skills:

1. Identify personal internal and external time wasters and ways you management them. Share these with your preceptee.

2. Be a time management role model for your preceptee. Share your rationale for strategies with your preceptee.

3. Collaborate with your preceptee to identify his or her time wasters, particularly those that are most important to target for change first.

4. Help the preceptee prioritize activities.

5. As events occur during the shift that challenge your preceptee's ability to organize, share your reasoning with your preceptee as you assist in reorganization.

6. Be sure to point out the commonly occurring time-related events that occur on your unit. Include any ways the team is involved in managing these events.

7. Avoid criticizing your preceptee. Instead, offer suggestions for changes in behavior.

8. Encourage questions and help the preceptee answer his or her own questions when appropriate.

9. Check on prioritization and organization periodically throughout the shift. Help with making necessary changes.

10. When unexpected or emergent events occur, help the preceptee with the event and with reorganizing.

11. Help preceptee anticipate events and organize to manage them.

12. Assist preceptee in identifying appropriate situations for delegation.

13. Model and help the preceptee find ways of dealing with time-wasting situations such as patients, families, and visitors. Identify ways of "trading time" to stay in control of time.

14. Coach the preceptee in identifying ways to manage time while collaborating with other staff or departments.

15. Encourage reflection about events in the shift and ways of improving time management to help the preceptee identify what time management strategies worked and what ones should be changed to improve effectiveness.

16. Track your preceptee's progressing improvement and share them with your preceptee (see **Form 5-3**).

17. If your preceptee is experienced, focus on time management as it relates to specifics on your unit. Let the preceptee's behaviors guide how you proceed. Being overly directive will probably not be helpful.

Summary

This chapter describes strategies for helping a preceptee develop time management skills. For new nurses or student nurses, time management is a particular problem, so ways of dealing with these problems are included. In addition, classic internal and external time wasters are described as well as strategies for dealing with each of these time thieves.

Reflection

• Refer to the section in the beginning of this chapter called Questions to Guide Your Learning. After completing this chapter, see if you can answer the questions. Some suggested answers are included in Appendix A.

- Think about your preceptee's time management skills. Identify improvements that have occurred. What plans do you have for helping with continued improvement? Is your preceptee able to identify improvements that have occurred? If not, it would be helpful to point out improvements you have observed. Encourage the preceptee to develop plans for further improvement.

- Are there other beginning nurses being precepted in your agency? You might explore the possibility of organizing a group of them to discuss time management issues and successful strategies that have worked. You may also want to meet with other preceptors in your agency to explore others' strategies and frustrations.

References

Ahmad, S. (2007). *Deal with time wasters for effective time management.* Retrieved February 19, 2008, from http://ezinearticles.com/?Deal-with-Time-Wasters-for-Effective-Time-Management&id=552818

American Nurses Association and the National Council of State Boards of Nursing. (2007). *Joint statement.* Retrieved February 19, 2008, from https://www.ncsbn.org/pdfs/Joint_statement.pdf

Chang, K., & Lutes, K. (n.d.). *The iCare worksheet.* Retrieved February 19, 2008, from http://www.purdue.edu/dp/energize04/posters/icare.pdf

Davenport, C. B. (n.d.). *What nurses need to know about personal digital assistants (PDAs).* Retrieved February 19, 2008, from http://www.eaa-knowledge.com/ojni/ni/8_3/davenport.htm

Gran-Moravec, M., & Hughes, C. (2005). Nursing time allocation and other considerations for staffing. *Nursing and Health Sciences, 7,* 126–133.

Hudspeth, R. (2007). Understanding delegation is a critical competency for nurses in the new millennium. *Nursing Administration Quarterly, 31,* 183–184.

Lacey, L., & Shaver, K. (2002). *Reductions in the amount of time spent in direct patient care by staff nurses in North Carolina: Findings from the 2001 survey of staff nurses in North Carolina.* Retrieved February 19, 2008, from http://www.ga.unc.edu/NCCN/research/chgs_time_alloctn.pdf

Pierce, C. (2006). Ten steps to effective delegation. *Nursing Management, 13,* 19.

Waterworth, S. (2003). Time management strategies in nursing practice. *Journal of Advanced Nursing, 43,* 432–440.

Williams, K. M. (n.d.). *Tips on effective time management.* Retrieved February 19, 2008, from http://ohioline.osu.edu/cd-fact/1006.html

NOTES

_____

_____

_____

_____

_____

_____

_____

_____

_____

_____

_____

_____

_____

_____

_____

_____

_____

_____

_____

_____

FORM 5-1: ACTIVITY RECORD

Time	Activity Description	Planned or Unplanned Activity

FORM 5-2: SAMPLE WORKSHEET

Room #	TX:	Neuro:	T:	T:	
Name:		Resp:	P:	P:	
DX:		CardioVasc:	R:	R:	
HX		Extremities:	BP:	BP:	
REPORT		GI / GU	Intake:	Output:	
MED'S AM		Skin	Teaching		
MED'S\ PM		Pain:			
IV		OTHER:			
MD'S	LABS				
ALLERGY	ABNORMAL LABS				
ACTIVITY					
DIET					

FORM 5-3: TRACKING PRECEPTEE TIME MANAGEMENT IMPROVEMENTS

Time Management Problem	Collaborative Plan for Improving	Observed Improvement

CHAPTER SIX

Facilitating Adult Learning and a Variety of Learning Styles

The teacher, if he is indeed wise, does not bid you to enter the house of wisdom but leads you to the threshold of your own mind.

—Kahlil Gibran

INTRODUCTION

Learning is affected by developmental levels, what is being learned, and how one prefers to take in information and then process it. As someone who is working to facilitate learning in a preceptee, it is important to know principles and models of ways to enhance how your preceptee learns. In this chapter we explore some principles of adult learning (your preceptee's developmental level) and differences in learning styles. Keep in mind that how you best learn may be very different from your preceptee's preferred learning approaches. When differences exist it is helpful to alter teaching strategies to facilitate your preceptee's learning. You will explore strategies to facilitate adult learning as well as strategies appropriate for differences in learning styles. You may even gain some insights into your own learning styles and what motivates you to learn.

OBJECTIVES

After completing the chapter and related learning activities, you should be able to

1. Describe elements of learning.
2. Describe Knowles assumptions of adult learning.
3. Describe preceptor approaches that apply Knowles assumptions to facilitate learning.
4. Describe Kolb's Learning Style model.
5. Describe preceptor strategies that apply Kolb's learning style model to facilitate learning.

6. Describe Felder's five learning style dimensions; opposing ways of taking in information and of processing information.

7. Using the information gained from the scores on Felder's Inventory of Learning Styles, describe appropriate preceptor strategies.

8. Describe your own learning style preferences as revealed on the Felder Inventory results.

9. Describe your preceptee's learning style preferences.

10. Develop (describe) preceptor approaches that facilitate preceptee learning styles.

QUESTIONS TO GUIDE YOUR LEARNING

1. Your preceptee has had three patients who had particularly challenging behavior management problems. With each patient, she analyzed factors that seemed to underlie the patients' behaviors and then found ways of interacting with the patients in ways that stopped the patients' challenging actions. Has this person learned? What elements of the definition of learning are present or not present in this situation?

2. What is one preceptor strategy that applies each of Knowles' five principles of adult learning to the precepting situation?

3. What are two characteristics of each of Kolb's four learning styles?

4. In Kolb's and Felder's learning style models, what is the importance of preferred learning style strength?

5. What are the characteristics of each of Felder's four dimensions of learning preference?

6. What is one preceptor strategy that would facilitate learning for each of Felder's four dimensions of learning styles?

7. What are your learning style preferences and your preceptee's learning style preferences?

Learning Defined

This chapter focuses on learning. Let's start by defining what that is. Learning is defined as a new or a change, that is relatively permanent, in knowledge and/or behavior (which can be intentional or unintentional, bad or good) that occurs as a result of interaction with the environment and experience of some kind. It does not describe change that occurs because of maturation or because of temporary conditions such as illness or fatigue (Woolfolk, 2001).

Knowles and Adult Learning

Let's start with adult learning and how you can use what you know about how adults like to learn while working with your preceptee. Using adult-appropriate approaches should enhance your preceptee's skill development progress. Knowles' assumptions of adult learning are described as well as ways you can apply his assumptions when working with your preceptee. Keep in mind that the preceptee needs to spend some time working with you and the situations occurring on the unit to learn your roles and his or her roles. So, for example, one adult learning assumption is that the adult wants to be self-directing, but this will not happen the moment you start working with the preceptee. It occurs with experiences, over time.

Knowles' Five Adult Learning Assumptions

Knowles (1984) described five assumptions about adult learners that he proposed were different from how younger people learn.

1. Adults are increasingly independent and self-directed. They tend to resist situations that do not allow self-direction.

    The new nurse wants to achieve in the professional role, so there is motivation to gain the knowledge and skills needed for the role. Preceptees have varying degrees of self-direction depending on the preceptee's past experiences with learning (being told versus discovering new concepts), self-concept, confidence, and previous experiences with what is to be learned as well as your approaches to the preceptee's learning. If supported, preceptees wanting to become independent should become more self-directed in setting their own goals, locating resources, making decisions, and taking actions (Brookfield, 1986, 1996).

    Preceptor strategies related to assumption 1 include the following:

    - Collaborate with the preceptee to identify learning needs and directions to be taken. For example, you can spend a short time at the end of a shift making plans with your preceptee for working on skills for the next shift.

    - As the preceptee gains experience in his or her roles with you, facilitate learning but support increasing self-direction. Encourage your preceptee to make decisions about what and how he or she wants to learn; guide the preceptee in discovering knowledge rather than supplying it when possible. You might, for example, ask the preceptee what they need to know for today and what resources they might need to acquire the information.

2. Readiness to learn is influenced by the need to know or to be able to do something to achieve in roles.

    Frequently, one will see nurses in the 20- to 30-year age range selecting critical care and emergent care as their preferred clinical area. Similarly, students and new nurses with young families may choose clinical situations in which children are being treated, and those who have had recent personal experiences with cancer or heart disease might opt for placement in those areas. A preceptee's learning is enhanced if teaching strategies include acknowledgment of the preceptee's life stage and her or his life objectives as well as goals.

Adult readiness to learn is determined by the preceptee's developmental state and resultant tasks to be accomplished. Differences in maturation, task accomplishments, and cognitive ability influence both what is learned and the rate of learning. Learning needs often become secondary to the preceptee's responsibility to family, job, and community.

Because adult learners perceive themselves as achievers, they want to be treated with respect. They avoid situations in which they have little control. They do not want to be told what they can and cannot do, be demeaned, or be prejudged. Adult learners learn best in an environment that does not threaten their self-concept and self-esteem.

Adults want to know why they should learn something; they want to know how a new skill, knowledge, or attitude is important. Adults need a reason for learning something rather than just memorizing something because someone indicated that need.

Preceptor strategies related to assumption 2 include the following:

- Requirements of taking on a new independent role stimulate preceptee readiness to learn. The preceptee is motivated to perform safely and appropriately. Remember to help the preceptee make the connection between what you might be teaching and a clear view of how learning this will help in role performance.

- Be sure the preceptee has a clear perception of rationale for learning. Show how what will be learned is applicable to roles being developed. You could just tell preceptees how they will use a piece of information or how he or she will be using particular laboratory results. You could also help the preceptee discover what knowledge is needed. Ask the preceptee how the information you are providing might be used.

- Be sure to relate experience goals (daily, weekly, or end goals) to objectives. If you and the preceptee have established an objective for the next shift, be sure the preceptee understands how this applies to skill progression and how doing this helps to increase skills.

- Be sensitive to the possibility that your preceptee's current responsibilities and living background events may affect learning readiness and the quality of participation in learning activities. If a child is sick at home or if the preceptee was up late working another job, motivation for learning will probably be compromised by the need for sleep or the need to take care of the sick child.

- Avoid demeaning criticizing approaches with your preceptee. Think of how you would want to be treated if you were sent to a new unit that was quite different from yours, or how you would want your manager or supervisor to treat you. Positive feedback and reinforcement enhances motivation and learning.

3. Experiences that adults bring to situations provide a base and resources for their learning.

Adults have accumulated life experiences and knowledge derived from work, family, and previous education. New experiences are received or experienced in terms of integration with past knowledge and experiences. It is important to relate or make relevant what is being learned to these accumulated experiences and to prior knowledge. For example, if your preceptee worked as a licensed vocational nurse before returning for a professional degree in nursing, you should explore the knowledge and skills already acquired and then proceed from the known to more complex endeavors. It would be inappropriate to proceed as if there had been no previous experiences.

Presuppositions and biases can be attached to past experiences. These may interfere with and certainly color learning. It is important to be acquainted with the preceptee's experiences that are influencing current behavior.

Preceptor strategies related to assumption 3 are as follows:

- Be sure to consult with your preceptee about his or her past experiences. Use these in collaborating with the preceptee to plan for new learning. Explore areas where there have been many experiences and few experiences. Also, use past experiences to clarify biases or values that may influence preceptee actions.

- Involve the learner in setting goals and objectives. Encourage your preceptee to make plans that facilitate progression by building on past experiences.

- In new situations, encourage reflection about similarities with past experiences. You might ask, "What was similar about this experience today to something that has happened with you in the past?" or "Should this happen again, what would you do differently?"

- As you work with your preceptee and learn about various past experiences, relate what was learned in those experiences to what is being learned now.

4. The orientation to learning includes problem-solving and knowledge-seeking behaviors motivated by the need to develop skills that are immediately applicable to real-life situations.

Adults want to solve problems and apply their new knowledge immediately. They tend not to learn just for the sake of learning. Active experiential learning using real-life situations enhances learning. The clinical setting is well suited to fostering the preferred problem-solving approaches and immediate application needs. You don't need to worry that you are only expecting your preceptee to learn tasks or facts. They are actually applying knowledge and skills in a real setting. Your role is to guide and facilitate problem solving. Your preceptee will have an attitude of "What do I need to know to get through today," not "Today I need to know *all* of the common procedures used on this unit."

Preceptor strategies related to assumption 4 are as follows:

- Concentrate on providing for learning experiences most useful for the preceptee at the time. For instance, you might have just attended a course on utilization review. The preceptee will probably not be receptive to instruction regarding what you have learned about utilization review when he or she is desperately trying to understand the properties of hemodynamic monitoring because this is what demands his or her most immediate attention.

- Plan for adding experiences that you can predict the preceptee will need almost immediately before those experiences that may or may not occur. Involve the preceptee in this planning. Use a problem-centered approach to facilitate learning, being sure your preceptee can relate usefulness of what is to be learned to current or anticipated problems. Questioning and prompting thinking should help to develop this habit. For example, if a preceptee had a patient who was post–coronary artery bypass surgery, you might ask, "What responses to this patient's surgery are most important to note" or "What is the importance of Mrs. C.'s low potassium level." You might also ask, "What might you anticipate happening because of Mrs. C.'s low potassium?"

- Provide for applied learning experiences. Find an opportunity for application of something you have instructed soon after the instruction. This reinforces the preceptee's learning and increases the chances that the preceptee can recall the instruction.

- Provide feedback on performance soon after the preceptee applies something you instructed. Providing rapid and rich feedback helps the preceptee remember the situation and meet the need for immediate application. It is important to provide objective specific observations of performance rather than your judgment about the behavior. For example, an objective observation is, "Anne, I observed you set a cup of coffee on the top of the computer." This statement describes a behavior and affords Anne the opportunity to validate or refute the observation. A judgmental observation is, "Anne, how dumb can you be? If that coffee spills, it could ruin the expensive computer equipment." In this case Anne would become immediately defensive in response to your personal attack on her.

5. Adults are motivated to learn by internal factors such as confidence or self-esteem rather than by external pressures or rewards like raises or promotions.

It does not motivate adults to tell them they have to change or to pressure them to learn something. Adults want to learn when they understand that learning will help them achieve in role or goal achievement. Frequently, a change in life roles prompts the need to learn. These changes can be events like divorce, moving to a different area, or children leaving home. Some sources of motivation for adult learning include a desire for social relationships like wanting to make new friends or relate to others in some way, a desire for personal advancement, escape a situation such as relieving boredom, pursuing a cognitive interest, and participating in social welfare (Leib 1991).

You probably already have a motivated learner; however, the events described above may influence performance during the precepting experience. Your teaching role is not one of initiating and motivating the learner. Your role is more one of removing or reducing obstacles to learning and enhancing the process.

Preceptor strategies related to assumption 5 include the following:

- Provide feedback and positive reinforcement about what is being learned.

- Establish an environment of trust between you and the preceptee. Promote your preceptee's feelings of adequacy, competency, and security.

- Be sure the preceptee sees a need to learn in particular situations.

- Minimize barriers to learning, for example, being sure the preceptee is able to manage assignments, adding new learning experiences at a pace in which a learner is able to achieve, and facilitating learner participation in planning for learning.

Learning Style Models

In addition to knowing about adult learning preferences and how to use that information, it is also helpful to know that adults have different preferences for ways of learning. Learners have different preferred ways of taking in information, such as verbally or visually, and for processing that information, like manipulating something or thinking about details before acting. They could learn using a variety of modes; however, in their preferred mode learning tends to proceed faster and more easily for the learner (Kolb, 1999). There are a number of learning style models in the literature; however, two prominent models are described here: the Kolb and Felder learning style models. Each model is described along with teaching strategies that tend to appeal to differing styles.

Kolb Learning Style Model

Kolb (1999) described individuals as having different ways of taking in information (grasping or understanding) and then of processing the information (sorting it out or transforming it into meaning). He described further that people have varying degrees of preferences for two different ways of taking in or understanding information by either *concrete experiences* (doing) or *abstract conceptualization* (thinking). If the learner has a preference for taking in information through concrete experience, this learner likes having specific experiences, experiences with the environment, and from other people and through feelings. If, on the other hand, the learner has a preference for taking in information through abstract conceptualization, this learner likes thinking about or analyzing ideas or situations. After grasping the information concretely or abstractly, people then have varying degrees of preference for two different ways of processing or making meaning of that information. The two ways are either *reflective observation*, in which the learner reflects about the information by watching and listening, by observing before making judgments, or looking at the information from several perspectives, or *active experimentation*, in which the learner learns by doing, acting out, or performing in the situation and influences others through actions.

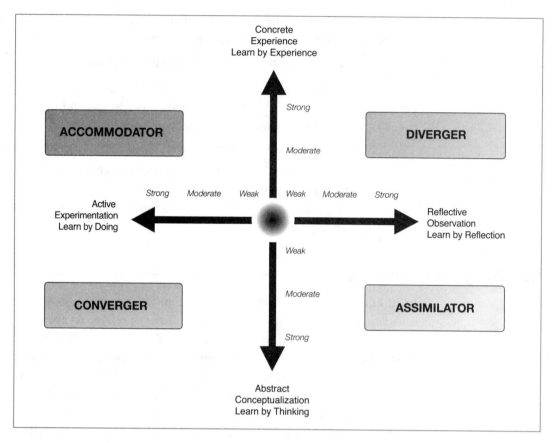

Figure 6-1. Kolb's learning style model.
Adapted from Kolb, D. A. (1999). *Learning style inventory: Version 3*. Boston: McBer & Co.

Keep in mind that there are differing degrees or strengths for these preferences. Some people have relatively weak preferences for some or all modes; they seem to be balanced in their approaches between ways of taking in and processing information. However, if they have strong preferences for one way or another, their learning can be facilitated if their preferred ways are present in the learning situation.

Kolb describes four different learning styles that consist of a combination of the preferences for the four dimensions of taking in and processing information. He calls these styles *diverging, converging, assimilating,* and *accommodating.* You may recognize them in yourself and in your preceptee. See **Figure 6-1** for a graphic view of the Kolb model.

Diverging and Converging Learning Styles

When one has a preference for the combination of concrete experience and reflective observation (one who reflects concretely), this is a diverging style. A diverger tends to take in information through concrete experiences, like working with others in situations and processing experiences through reflective observation. The diverger probably likes gathering information and generating different ideas (think of this learning style as diverging from just one way of looking at situations); however, the diverger does *not* focus on taking action.

When one has a preference for the combination of abstract conceptualization and active experimentation, this is a converging style (a thinking doer). This is a polar opposite of the diverging style. Learners with this style take in information through abstract conceptualization, but rather than reflecting this learner goes ahead and takes action. Whereas divergers tend to like working with people/others, the converger tends to like working alone. The converger focuses on solving a problem and finding a solution, whereas the diverger likes to think of possibilities and consequences more extensively before taking action to solve problems.

Can you see yourself as being more like a diverger or more like a converger? What if your preceptee is more like the opposite style? You could make each other crazy or at least have some frustrations when approaching and working in some situations. On the other hand, you could use each other's strengths. If you liked to reflect about several possibilities but not tend to make decisions, you could benefit by a converger's tendency to make decisions and take action. Also, your tendency to reflect about possibilities will come in handy for holding back on decisions that are too fast or risky.

Accommodating and Assimilating Learning Styles

The accommodator has a preference for the combination of concrete experience and active experimentation (a concrete doer). This learner takes in information through specific (hands on) experiences and processes it through active experimentation. This learner likes to act and to carry out plans and may solve problems by intuition or trying out different things rather than logical analysis. This learner tends to take more risks. Is this your style?

The assimilator prefers the combination of taking in information abstractly and processing it via reflective observation (an abstract reflector). This learner is interested in abstract ways of looking at things, is good at organizing many ideas and observations into an integrated whole, and likes it when things are logically precise and everything fits. Like the converger, this learner prefers working alone. Is this more like you?

Again, this style tends to be a polar opposite of the accommodator. The assimilator takes in information by abstract conceptualization, whereas the accommodator prefers concrete experience. The assimilator processes information by reflecting, whereas the accommodator prefers processing by doing.

Kolb Cycle of Learning

Kolb indicates that learning preferences may vary depending on the content and the situation. Kolb also believes that an individual may start learning by using any one of the four processes and then, with experience, cycle through all of them. An example of a cycle might be the beginner learning how to give a useful report. The beginner may start by watching you give report or trying to do it alone (concrete experience). The beginner could add to this by thinking about characteristics of your report compared with others (reflective observation). After more experience the learner may start thinking about the various pieces of information that should be in a good report (abstract conceptualization). Next, the learner may refine and practice his or her skill giving a report (active experimentation). See **Table 6-1** for a summary of Kolb's learning styles.

Preceptor Strategies Related to the Kolb Learning Style Model

How can you use what you've learned about Kolb's learning styles? As you look at the descriptions of these learners, what learning style do you prefer? Do you like to learn best when you are learning something that is concrete or do you like to analyze things? After you understand something, do you like to do something active with it or think about several potential aspects and consequences of various choices? Consider exploring your preceptee's

Table 6-1. Kolb Learning Style Model Summary	
Style: Combined Ways of Taking in and Processing Information	**Distinguishing Tendencies**
Diverging Learn through concrete experience and reflection	Likes unambiguous experiences Likes working with others Gathers information and thinks about possibilities and ideas Sensitive to feelings Not focused on taking action
Assimilating Learn by thinking (abstract concepts) and reflection	Organizes ideas and observations into an integrated whole Likes things to be logically precise Likes working alone; more focused on concepts and ideas than people
Converging Learn by thinking (abstract concepts) and doing	Thinks about and analyzes information Focuses gathered information on problem solving and finding practical solutions Takes action based on decided solutions Likes working alone
Accommodating Learn through concrete experience and by active manipulation	Likes specific hands-on experiences and processes Acts on plans more intuitively or just trying out things than on logical analysis May take risks and act without careful consideration

learning preferences (see **Form 6-1**). If they are similar to yours, you can approach teaching in ways that you like to learn. If they are different, both you and the preceptee may need to negotiate some alterations in the ways you approach learning. This stretching is not easy. It takes time to learn and change to differing ways of learning. It's a bit like wearing your shoes on the wrong feet; particularly if your preferences are strong. The following strategies may help:

- Discuss learning preferences with your preceptee. Work with your preceptee to find preferred ways of taking in and processing information. Pay attention to the strength of the preference. For example, if your preceptee says "I won't remember this until I do it," this tells you there is a relatively strong preference for active experimentation. Keep in mind, however, that a preferred style may change as situations change and as the learner has experiences in recurring situations.

  If the two of you have strong opposing preferences you can still work together. It just may slow the learning process. You can probably negotiate collaborative style modifications. Both of you may need to make changes or be tolerant and understanding of your differences. If this doesn't work and you just can't deal with your preceptee, you might consider a different preceptee if this is a possibility. Your manager may not have considered your differences or known of them when placing the preceptee with you. If a faculty member placed a student with you, speak with the faculty liaison about placing a different student with you.

- It may help if you only realize your differences and allow your learner to use his or her own preferred ways when possible. This could work if the strength of preferences is not very strong. For example, your preceptee may need to understand detailed rationale for some procedures. You, on the other hand, don't focus on these details; you may have known them way back, but you have not used them in a while. You could assist your preceptee in looking up the rationale.

- If you have differing styles, you can use each other's learning strengths. For example, if you like to act after grasping some information with little or no analyzing but your preceptee likes to think about it and generate ideas before acting, you could use this strength from time to time. As well, the preceptee can try to use your model of making decisions and taking action a little faster.

Felder-Silverman Learning Style Model

Another learning style model, the Felder-Silverman learning style model (Felder, 1993), describes four dichotomous learning style dimensions: *sensing/intuitive, visual/verbal, active/reflective,* and *sequential/global.* The first two dichotomies are preferences for taking in information. The last two focus on preferences for ways to process information. Each of the dimensions is represented on a continuous scale of varying preference strengths. For example, a person could have between a weak, moderate, or strong preference for one or the other side of each dichotomy. See **Figure 6-2** for an example of one person's score on the visual/verbal dimension. In this example, a score of 7 indicates a relatively strong preference

Figure 6-2. Example of where one person might score on Felder's visual/verbal learning style dimension.

for taking in (perceiving) information visually. If this same person had a score of 3 or 1 on the visual side of the continuum, a relatively weak preference is indicated. This person is more balanced in preference and could more easily take in information either visually or verbally than someone with a score of 7 or 11. Each of the four dimensions is described in more detail below.

Sensing and Intuitive Dimension

This dimension involves preferences for ways of perceiving information more by sensing (sights, sounds, physical sensations) or more by intuition (insights, ideas, memories, discerning, imagining) (Felder, 1993). Learners who are strong to moderate sensors like predictable concrete experiences, facts, details, and active manipulation. Those learners who have a strong to moderately strong preference for intuition like more abstract ideas, innovation, variety, and exploring ideas.

Visual and Verbal Dimension

This dimension involves other preferred ways of taking in information. In this case there can be a preference more for visual (pictures, diagrams demonstrations) or more for verbal information (written and spoken words) (Felder, 1993). A strong or moderately strong visual learner would have relative difficulty processing and remembering when the only way of taking in information is someone talking and giving verbal instruction or directions. A strong or moderately strong verbal learner would be able to take in information relatively easily from a lecture or verbal directions. The last two dimensions describe preferences for processing information.

Active and Reflective Dimension

In this dimension learners prefer to process information more actively (physical activity, manipulation, trying things out, discussion) or more reflectively (thinking about, analyzing). It's important for the active learner to directly engage in learning, whereas the reflective learner prefers to think about things first.

Sequential and Global Dimension

These learners prefer to progress in processing information more sequentially (using small progressive steps, working with details) or more globally (dealing with the big picture, seeing things holistically). The global learner may get confused by too much detail, whereas the sequential learner may need help in seeing the big picture.

Preceptor Strategies Related to Felder's Learning Style Model

Although it is difficult to match your preceptee's learning style, you should at least be aware that you will tend to teach in a manner that uses your preferences in style, which probably influences learning. Instead, you may try to stretch some into the opposing dimension. For example, if you had a preference for thinking and reflecting and your preceptee was a strong active learner, it would be helpful to let this learner do something active related to what is to be learned and then proceed more toward your reflecting approach.

Refer again to the strategies suggested for Kolb's styles. Some other preceptor strategies are described below. Keep in mind that each of the preferences may vary in strength and with various situations. Both you and your preceptee should try to stretch into opposing dimensions. Some preceptees are balanced in all dimensions and can learn well in all dimensions, so stretching wouldn't be necessary.

- Explore your preferred styles and your preceptee's preferences. See http://www.engr.ncsu .edu/learningstyles/ilsweb.html and take the 44-question inventory to discover your and your preceptee's learning style preferences (Felder & Soloman, n.d.).

- Felder (1993) suggested that learning is facilitated when strategies appeal to a variety of the dimensions. He proposed that strategies like lecturing or telling (you sharing what you know with the learner) works well for the intuitive, verbal, reflective, and sequential preferences; so if you add other learning experiences to these approaches you will be using styles that appeal to the sensing, visual, active, and global learners.

  - Give an overview of what is to be learned and then specific examples that illustrate how the material can be used (global, sensing).

  - In addition to written and oral information, use sketches, diagrams, or physical demonstrations (visual).

  - In addition to conceptual information, include concrete descriptions (sensing).

  - In addition to encouraging thinking about what has happened (reflective), provide opportunities for your preceptee to actively participate by trying something out, or asking questions, or explaining it to you (active).

- If you have an active learner preceptee, encourage discussions about what is being learned, let the learner try things out, and practice skills rather than reading about them in the procedure manual.

- If your preceptee favors reflection, encourage reflection about events occurring in the learning experiences. For example, you could encourage journaling about experiences.

- Providing real-world examples is helpful for sensing learners.

- Providing too much detail may interfere with learning for the intuitor. The intuitor also may work fast but make mistakes. Encourage checking for accuracy.

- If your preceptee prefers visual input, try to use demonstration, diagrams, or pictures rather than just talking about something.

- If your preceptee has a preference for verbal input, provide for discussion, written material, and talking about the day's events.

- If the preceptee has a sequential preference, be sure each step in what you are teaching follows from a previous step (go step by step). If you tend to jump around when you explain things, try to list out the needed learning steps so you don't forget.

- If the preceptee prefers a more global approach to processing information, try to give an overview or help the preceptee link disjointed understandings into a big picture. You can detect this when you see the insight ("light bulb turning on") in a learner, when suddenly the learner "gets it" because they have put the pieces all together into a bigger understanding of events.

Preceptor Strategies

Working with Beginning Nurses

Several strategies have been suggested for adult learning preferences and for two learning style models. Refer back to these strategies. Here is a general summary:

1. Encourage and allow your preceptee to become increasingly self-directed.

2. Be sure your preceptee understands the importance of knowing or developing a skill to her or his practical use. Do this for everything you are introducing as you teach the preceptee.

3. Assess your preceptee's experiences that may apply to what is being learned. Relate, in some way, what is being learned to your preceptee's experiences.

4. Support your preceptee's growing confidence. Provide constructive feedback about what is being learned.

5. Discuss learning preferences with your preceptee. Try to identify preferred ways of taking in and processing information. Remember strength of preference varies.

6. Try to use your preceptee's and your own learning strengths to facilitate learning progression.

7. Use a variety of teaching strategies (demonstration, written directions, discussions, questioning, diagrams, pictures, journaling, etc.) that may appeal to different style preferences.

Working with the Experienced Nurse

Learning style implications for you and your preceptee described above apply to your experienced nurse in much the same manner. Here they are reviewed:

1. With experience it is even more important to assess and respond to your preceptee's past experiences so you can adjust your approaches to use those experiences as you facilitate progression.

2. Habits of self-direction probably occur more rapidly than with new nurses or students. Be sure to let go of your control and even encourage progression toward increasing self-direction.

3. If your preceptee has had considerable experience, particularly in settings similar to yours, adjusting to differing learning styles may be easier. Always collaborate with the preceptee, assess learning preferences, and make plans for ways of responding to them.

Summary

This chapter describes adult learning characteristics and two learning style models along with related preceptor strategies that facilitate learning. Remember that your preferred learning approaches may be different from your preceptee's so that you may need to alter your strategies as you work together. Also, remember that most of the learners you will be working with are able to learn in each of the differing modes described. It is just easier for them to take in and process information in preferred ways. Recall that the preferences vary in strength, with the content to be learned, and with situations in which they are being learned, including the learner's past experience with similar situations. You may want to use **Form 6-1** to assess learning preferences and associated facilitative preceptor strategies.

Reflection

- Refer to the section in the beginning of this chapter called Questions to Guide Your Learning. After completing this chapter, see if you can answer the questions. Some suggested answers are included in Appendix A.

- Think about something you learned recently. In what way did the three elements listed below contribute to your success?
  - Learner factors, such as your past experiences with the topic or skill, including previously acquired knowledge, and your motivation
  - Teacher factors, which relate to how the teacher facilitated learning and what strategies the teacher used that helped you learn
  - What was learned, for example, the topic or subject matter

- Think of another thing you learned recently. What motivated you to learn that? What motivates your preceptee?

- If adults' readiness to learn is influenced by their need to know or to be able to do something, what is one way you might influence your preceptee's need to manage the care of five patients.

- One assumption about adult learning is that it is motivated by internal factors such as confidence or self-esteem. Describe one preceptor strategy that would appeal to internal factors of confidence?

- Knowles assumes that adult learners want to be self-directed. Describe one example of encouraging self-direction.

- How do your preceptee's past experiences influence interactions between the two of you?

- Your adult learner wants to seek knowledge and skills that are immediately useful in real situations. Describe one preceptor strategy that applies this desire?

- Decide about your preferences for opposite learning styles (assimilating or accommodating, diverging or converging). What drives you nuts when trying to learn something? For example, jumping in to take action without much thought as opposed to thinking about it and observing factors and considering things from all angles. How could you accommodate to your opposite preference?

- What is one situation when it would be good to have a preferred learning style of a converger?

- What are your learning style preferences in Kolb's model and in Felder's model? What are your preceptee's preferences?

- You are a person who likes to pick up a piece of new equipment and just figure out how to make it work. Your preceptee wants to read the directions and follow them step by step. How do you respond to this need?

- You are an assimilator. You work with an accommodating preceptee. Your preceptee gets frustrated with all the details you include in instructions. What is one thing you could do to appeal to your preceptee's preferred approach?

- You have a preference for the converging style of learning. Do you like working alone or with others? What does your preceptee prefer?

- How does your preceptee prefer to take in new information: by sensing or by intuition or by visual or verbal? Are these preferences strong, moderate, or weak? How do your preferences compare with your preceptee? How does this influence your approaches?

- According to Felder, of the preferred ways of processing information, active or reflective, sequential or global, what are your preferences? What are your preceptee's preferences? In each case, are these preferences strong, moderate, or weak? How do you respond to differences?

- Felder proposes that lecturing or telling (you sharing what you know with the learner) tends to support learners who have intuitive, verbal, reflective, and sequential preferences for learning. If you are trying to teach your preceptee using strategies that appeal to a variety of styles, other than telling, what two strategies might you use to appeal to learners with sensing, visual, active, and global preferred ways of learning?

References

Brookfield, S. (1986). *Understanding and facilitating adult learning.* San Francisco: Jossey-Bass.

Brookfield, S. (1996). Adult learning: An overview. In A. Tuinjman (Ed.), *International encyclopedia of adult education* (2nd ed., pp. 375–380). Oxford: Pergamon Press.

Felder, R. (1993). Reaching the second tier: Learning and teaching styles in college science education. *Journal of College Science Teaching, 23,* 286–290.

Felder, R., & Soloman, B. (n.d.). *Learning style inventory.* Retrieved September 7, 2007, from http://www.engr.ncsu.edu/learningstyles/ilsweb.html

Knowles, M. S. (1984). *Andragogy in action: Applying modern principles of adult learning.* San Francisco: Jossey-Bass.

Kolb, D. A. (1999). *Learning style inventory: Version 3.* Boston: McBer & Co.

Leib, S. (1991). *Principles of adult learning.* Retrieved February 19, 2008, from http://honolulu.hawaii.edu/intranet/committees/FacDevCom/guidebk/teachtip/adults-2.htm

Woolfolk, A. (2001). *Educational psychology* (8th ed.). Needham Heights, MA: Pearson Education.

NOTES

FORM 6-1: LEARNING STYLE PLANNER

Use this form as desired to assess your preceptee's preferred learning approaches and to plan for learning that responds to these approaches.

Assess your Preceptee's Learning Preferences

What Motivates Your Preceptee's Learning?

_____

_____

_____

Preferred Learning Styles

_____

_____

_____

Plan Strategies to Facilitate Learning

Collaborate with your preceptee to identify strategies that respond to preferences. Start with three or four objectives that both you and the preceptee will try. You can add more as you learn more about other preferences.

_____

_____

_____

_____

_____

_____

(continues)

FORM 6-1: LEARNING STYLE PLANNER (CONTINUED)

Implement Planned Strategies

Try on these strategies for a fit in style that supports learning. List what you are trying.

_____

_____

_____

_____

Evaluate Effectiveness of Planned Strategies

Collaborate with your preceptee to decide how well-planned strategies are working for both of you. Discuss how well your objectives are being achieved. Plan for added objectives and for changes in strategies.

_____

_____

_____

_____

_____

_____

CHAPTER SEVEN

Maintaining Your Preceptee's Motivation

It is interesting to notice how some minds seem almost to create themselves, springing up under every disadvantage, and working their solitary but irresistible way through a thousand obstacles.

—Washington Irving

INTRODUCTION

Why do some people keep performing at optimal levels while others fizzle? What is it that helps to maintain ones initiation, direction, intensity, and persistence in nursing during challenging times? How do you bridge the gap between idealism of nursing school and the realities of practice when precepting new nurses? The literature is replete with studies supporting various motivational strategies for managerial use that is focused on developing and maintaining a motivated workforce. Millions of dollars are spent annually on incentives to maximize retention and recruitment efforts. There is a pervasive thought that nurses are motivated by money and that, if given enough, the nurse will consistently perform outstanding work. Also, much has been written about the effects that the work environment has on one's level of motivation. Yet, given high salaries, incentive bonuses, and a supportive working environment, a large number of professional nursing positions remain unfilled. Little research discusses personal values and beliefs the nurse has about oneself and how these relate to the values and beliefs held about the nursing profession. This chapter provides you with insight on the concept of motivation. You will be exploring ways your preceptee thinks about the goals of the precepted experience. You may begin to understand why your preceptee chooses to learn the role of a nurse and how you influence your preceptee's motivation. You will also be able to implement strategies that may enhance your preceptee's initiation, sense of direction, intensity, and persistence of behavior with the process of expanding one's practice.

OBJECTIVES

After completing the chapter and related learning activities, you should be able to

1. Describe two basic components of motivation theory.
2. Describe two reasons why you remain employed as a nurse.
3. List two factors that motivated your preceptee to select a career in nursing.
4. Describe one challenge to your preceptee's values and beliefs during the decision-making process to become a nurse.
5. Describe one preceptor strategy that could minimize the values challenge that your preceptee may experience.
6. Describe one way in which your preceptee's nursing role expectations might be challenged.
7. Describe four strategies you might use to enhance your preceptee's motivation and feelings of safety while progressing professionally.
8. Define how motivation can alter one's performance.
9. Describe a strategy that will enhance your preceptee's ability to complete a challenging task effectively.

QUESTIONS TO GUIDE YOUR LEARNING

1. Why do you go to work? What motivates you to stay in a career that is fraught with challenges?
2. What advice would you give someone who is thinking about entering into nursing?
3. What strategies could help you motivate a preceptee who is internally motivated to enter into or to remain in nursing?
4. In what three ways do you plan to assist your preceptee achieve professional goals?
5. Your preceptee has a laundry list of things to be accomplished in a short period of time. You don't believe the list is achievable. What do you do?
6. How will you create a clinical learning environment that is safe for your preceptee?
7. What three things can you do to build autonomy in your preceptee?
8. What will you do if your preceptee shares feelings of being incapable to complete a certain task?

Commonalities Found in Motivation Theories

General constructs of motivational theory are discussed in this section. The models of two classic theorists are presented in an effort to provide you with a working level of knowledge that will benefit you personally and will help you as you work with your preceptee.

Motivation theories have blossomed since Pavlov sounded the bell that made his trusty pet dog salivate in anticipation of a food reward. However, structured research in motivation was initiated in 1954 when Abraham Maslow published his classic motivation model that is graphically displayed as five tiers of needs, commonly referred to as Maslow's Hierarchy of Needs. Basic needs are identified as physiological needs, such as the need for water, shelter, food, and comfort. As one's physiological needs are met, the next level in the hierarchy emerges relating to one's safety. These include the need for security, stability, and freedom from harm. Level three is structured around social needs, such as the need for friendship and belonging. The desires for self-respect and respect or recognition from others are represented at level four of Maslow's hierarchy, self-esteem. Finally, as all other needs are met, the individual is finally self-actualized, whereby the individual desires for self-fulfillment and the realization of one's full potential occurs (Maslow, 1970).

McClelland collapsed Maslow's hierarchy into three basic needs categories: the need for influence and power, the need for social interaction and affiliation, and the need for achievement (1971). Many contemporary theorists concur that there are personal, social, and achievement aspects that contribute to one's motivation. Whatever your theoretical affiliation or preference, the constructs of motivation remain basically the same: that motivation is a set of processes that moves a person toward a goal that is generated by need. As your experiences with your preceptee progress, you may find that your motivation for nursing and for the role of preceptor waxes and wanes, as may your preceptee's motivation to learn. Understanding motivation and being armed with strategies for enhancing motivation help you to work through the challenges you will face in your role as nurse and as preceptor.

What Motivates You and Your Preceptee?

There are infinite challenges associated with your role as a nurse. Undoubtedly, there were many times when you asked yourself why you became a nurse. How did you respond? What was your motivation? What sustains you today? How will you help your preceptee when the realities of the role set in?

Assessing Your Motivation to Remain in Nursing

Why did you become a nurse? Are you happy with your decision? How would you advise someone who is considering nursing as a professional career? To provide safe patient care, to acquire autonomy in practice, to have an opportunity for personal growth, and to have the ability to make a difference in people's lives are common factors that enhance job satisfaction among nurses. Do you concur with these motivators? How do you accomplish these in today's challenging healthcare environment? Reflect on your decision to become a nurse. Write your philosophy of nursing. What does nursing mean to you? How do you define health care? Who are healthcare consumers? And what constitutes a healthcare environment? Knowing your individual motivators assists you as you guide and support your preceptee through difficult situations that challenge even the most entrenched values and beliefs about nursing.

Assessing Your Preceptee's Motivation to Enter into Nursing Practice

There are three variables that are directly related to self-regulation and motivation when completing a goal such as a nursing task, a degree in nursing, or participating in a new graduate or new employee program. The first variable, a values component, reflects one's beliefs and values about the goal or task.

Values Component

When attempting to clarify beliefs about the importance and interest in a task, your preceptee might ask, "Why am I doing this?" Individual passion for achievement is fueled by both internal and external motivators. Internal motivation is the driving force that is personal in nature and is specific to the individual, such as that which drives personal satisfaction and enjoyment. External motivation is the force that influences individuals by those events or desires that are not personal to the individual. Examples of external motivators are rewards, money, and recognition. Coupled with internal and external motivation is the concept of mastery goals and performance goals.

Types of Goal Orientation

There are two basic types of goal orientation, mastery and performance. Mastery goals are those goals that direct learning because the individual seeks self-improvement regardless of the performance of others. Performance goals are set in a model of competition. Goal orientation predicts performance orientation. If your preceptee is mastery goal oriented, performance is highlighted by a positive attitude toward the task, skill, or achievement performed. Individuals seeking goal mastery generally self-monitor their progress toward achievement. They are able to relate previously learned material with new material, yielding greater comprehension of concept interrelatedness. In contrast, preceptees who are performance goal oriented tend to be rooted in memorization and rehearsal strategies. Critical-thinking and problem-solving skills tend be to less creative.

Reinforcement and confirmation from you is important for monitoring the degree of goal achievement. Researchers studied student's learning strategies and motivation for goal achievement by assessing their value of mastery as it relates to goal achievement. They found that when mastery of a goal was salient, students approached more challenging tasks with a positive attitude. Students used more effective strategies when completing the task and had stronger beliefs that success emanates from one's effort (Ames & Archer, 1988). A preceptee who becomes involved in a task or a job with mastery as the goal will enjoy the challenge and will be more receptive to differing strategies to promote mastery. Help your preceptee discover the importance and relevance associated with the assigned task. Doing so will assist your preceptee in valuing the task and its potential outcomes resulting in an increased future effort.

A second type of motivation stems from one's ability to perform a task. A belief in one's ability to achieve a goal or to perform a task also influences self-regulation and motivation. Those who believe they are capable of success in task achievement or goal attainment are more likely to use creative strategies and to demonstrate persistence toward achievement than those who believe they are less capable. Skills resulting from lower order thinking can be taught with skills requiring higher order thinking strategies. It was found that when taught together, tasks that are perceived to be elementary and not requiring much thought are better taught with more complex ideas within the context in which the learner will practice them (Shunk, 1989). Teaching a new skill within a context of reality assists your preceptee to see relationships between that which is learned and the environment in which it is applied. Creating opportunities for teaching and learning within the context of practice, including your preceptee as one of the team, and increasing your preceptee's level of power are all strategies that increase motivation to learn (Bradbury-Jones, Sambrook, & Irvine, 2007). For example, your hospital decides to switch from paper charts to electronic documentation. Teaching your preceptee to document patient assessment data electronically using the handheld technology in the patient's room during the assessment provides educational opportunities that are within the context of reality. You are also teaching time management and nurse–patient communication techniques. This strategy is more beneficial than teaching your preceptee to jot down assessment findings on a piece of paper and then to transcribe the data to the handheld electronic device outside the room at a later time.

Self-Concept and Beliefs of Attribution

Motivation and learning strategies are linked to one's self-concept of how performance is perceived and received by others. Social cognitive theorists purport that an individual's perceived efficacy frequently influences their motivation. Individuals who believe they have the capability for completing a specific task or skill usually choose to participate in more difficult situations, exert greater effort, persist longer, and develop creative problem-solving skills during the process.

Closely aligned with self-concept are attribution beliefs. Attribution deals with perceived causes of success. Is success correlated with ability, effort, task difficulty, or luck? Success increases self-confidence and self-efficacy in preceptees whose perceptions are that behavioral outcomes are related to effort and superior ability. They perceive they are responsible for the outcome of their actions. This is referred to as one's locus of control. Keep in mind that individual differences in locus of control affect how a job or task is approached. Those of us with an internal locus of control believe that our behavior has a direct effect on outcomes and that effort and reward are correlated. Those of us with an external locus of control believe there is little cause and effect relationship between individual control and outcome, that things "just happen." Preceptees who believe that outcomes are a byproduct of chance or fate alone do not experience feelings of success because they perceive they had no control over the situation. Preceptees who have an internal locus of control and who perceive that work, effort, and persistence influence outcomes tend to demonstrate greater motivation than those who do not. You may want to go online to http://www.ballarat.edu.au/ard/bssh/psych/RotterLOC.pdf (or any number of other sites) to complete an assessment to help both you and your preceptee determine individual locus of control, attributions, and self-efficacy. You can also learn a great deal about your preceptee's motivation by observing behaviors and exploring your preceptee's beliefs, values, and self-perceptions with respect to how a job or task is approached.

Influencing Your Preceptee's Motivation to Learn During the Precepting Experience

Goals are targets for action and thought. There are several characteristics of goals that enhance motivation. This section explores these characteristics and develops strategies to enhance your preceptee's plan for success.

Goal Setting

It is important to understand characteristics of goals before you assist your preceptee in setting the goals of the precepted learning experience. Preceptee behavior and motivation depend on goal specificity, proximity, and level of difficulty. Goals that are specific and set specific standards are more motivating than goals that demonstrate achievement in general terms. For instance, "successfully complete three intravenous starts" or "complete and document all assessments by 10 a.m." are more specific than "do my best at starting an intravenous line" or "complete my charting in a timely manner." The goals are clearly stated in the first two examples. The preceptee is able to determine the appropriate amount of effort required to achieve the goal. Subsequent success leads to increased satisfaction that in turn results in greater self-efficacy.

Proximal goals are more immediate and are not projected far into the future. Progression toward achieving proximal goals is more easily assessed when compared with progress toward distant goals. As an example, the goal of this text is to help you become a facilitative preceptor, a distant goal. However, your measurement of achievement is learning from and applying the strategies found within each chapter of the text. You're able to measure your progress and resulting success using proximal goals, thereby maintaining or increasing your motivation toward the more distant goal of becoming a facilitative preceptor.

Perception of task difficulty and the amount of effort required to complete a task influences motivation. If your preceptee believes he or she has the ability to achieve a task, skill, or job requirement, working hard to achieve a goal becomes less challenging. Increased levels of competence and personal satisfaction are the outcomes of goal achievement. Conversely, if there is a self-perception of a lack of ability to achieve or there are low expectations for success, a feeling of being overwhelmed can result, which then tends to reduce motivation.

Discussing both your and your preceptee's philosophies of nursing gives you valuable insight into what motivates your preceptee to choose nursing as a career. Actively listen for verbal indicators of intrinsic motivators, such as "I've always gained a great deal of satisfaction helping others," "nursing is my calling," or "I want to give back." These comments indicate your preceptee is motivated to become a nurse for personal reasons, reasons that come from within. Knowing this will assist you to effectively support and encourage your preceptee (Prater & McEwen, 2006).

Help your preceptee grow professionally by clearing the path for learning to occur. Anticipate opportunities from which your preceptee might benefit and create the environment for exposure to these opportunities. For example, if your preceptee is motivated by a "call to help ethnic mothers and their newborns," then your preceptee might be more motivated to work designing a bilingual booklet describing commonly asked questions of new moms during their first month postpartum instead of being assigned to the department's technology committee.

If your preceptee responds to your query with responses such as "nursing has finally gained respect as a profession," "nursing provides me with financial security," or "all the women in my family are nurses," anticipate that motivation is primarily governed by external variables. Coaching and providing support would be "best fit" strategies for your preceptee. Provide your preceptee with positive feedback, such as awarding your preceptee with a certificate of achievement or some other tangible reward. Create and maintain a learning environment where there is a great deal of social support.

Strategies to Enhance Goal Setting

- Help your preceptee divide proximal goals into smaller goals. Collaborate with your preceptee to establish the sequence for subgoals that enhance achievement and provide for feedback regarding progress. Achieving the smaller tasks enhances the chances for a positive outcome overall.

- Evaluate and validate that your preceptee's goals are attainable. Are they achievable? If the goals are too lofty, work with your preceptee to redevelop them so that chances for success are enhanced.

- Encourage self-assessment toward goal achievement. Self-monitoring helps to gain knowledge and to develop strategies that enhance the process of periodic goal assessments throughout one's professional career. Providing reliable and concise feedback helps to reestablish your preceptee's focus and to minimize challenges with the self-monitoring process.

- If you believe that your preceptee is not achieving planned goals, help by reevaluating and adjusting the timeline and the benchmarks for success.

- Encourage your preceptee to self-evaluate capabilities. Does your preceptee have the "right stuff" to succeed? Create opportunities for enhanced learning if your preceptee does not perceive having the ability to achieve.

Remember, progress enhances self-efficacy and self-efficacy is critical to developing and maintaining motivation.

Strategies for Creating a Safe Learning Environment Within the Complex Environment of Health Care

In a response to the growing number of indicators that unhealthy work environments contribute to increased medication errors, the inability to provide safe and effective care, and the cause of workplace strife among employees, the American Association of Critical

Care Nurses (2005) established standards for developing and sustaining healthy and safe work environments in acute and critical care settings. The constructs of the standards also apply to teaching and learning within the complex and demanding healthcare environment. The following are components that create a safe and professional learning environment.

Skilled Communication

Nurses communicate with many constituents in the course of a day. Interactive communication that promotes thought and quality decision making is the key element for skilled communication. Communication, whether it is written or spoken, should be respected and coveted. Value your preceptee's experience and expertise. Communication skills are as important to your preceptee's professional progression as acquiring technical skills.

True Collaboration

Grant your preceptee a voice. Give your preceptee the power and respect to participate collaboratively in decision making, planning, and conflict resolution so that optimal outcomes are achieved. Expect your preceptee to act with integrity. Anticipate that collaborative contributions will be made at the level of your preceptee's experience and knowledge.

Effective Decision Making

Your preceptee should be recognized as a valued and committed partner in making decisions. Help your preceptee develop feelings of accountability to enhance the development of an autonomous practice. Share your processes when planning, organizing, and assessing both at the clinical and at the organizational level so that your preceptee can learn how to make effective decisions that will guide professional practice.

Appropriate Assignments

Make certain that there is an effective match between patient needs and your preceptee's competencies. Expect your preceptee to provide high quality care and provide support to ensure that your preceptee successfully plans, organizes, and assesses patient care.

Meaningful Recognition

Recognition and reward is most effective when it is tailored to the individual. Recognize your preceptee's positive contributions and actions as often as possible. Realize that recognition is not an event but rather a form of feedback that is ongoing.

Authentic Leadership

Preceptors are leaders. In your preceptor role, it is expected that you demonstrate effective communication skills, you know how to motivate others in changing environments, you are committed to high standards of service, you are outcome oriented, and you model collaborative practice. Although it may seem daunting, it is expected that you teach your preceptee these roles through role modeling. Be enthusiastic in your leadership/preceptor role. Maintain both high standards and expectations for performance. Teach your preceptee to lead as capabilities allow. Following are preceptor strategies that may enhance motivation in beginning and experienced nurses.

Preceptor Strategies

Working with the Beginning Nurse

1. Use open communication techniques when collaborating with your preceptee. Communicate transparently. Have no hidden agendas.

2. Do what you say you're going to do. Actions speak louder than words, and the congruence between communication and action builds trust.

3. Speak to the point and do not engage in conversations that are less than positive. Doing so eliminates disrespectful behavior.

4. Ask for feedback regarding your communication skills from both your colleagues and your preceptee.

5. Support your preceptee's quest for knowledge. Find educational opportunities that are appropriate for your preceptee within your organization or offered by professional organizations to which you belong that facilitate skill acquisition.

6. Encourage your preceptee's presence at ethics committees and meetings where complex issues are discussed between the organization, care providers, patients, and their families. Your preceptee will be witness to the complexity of healthcare decisions and will have heightened awareness of constituent perspectives.

7. Model competency and ethics in your practice of nursing. Maintain a bar of idealism when providing care to those who are entrusted to you. Help your preceptee to develop a high standard of professional practice.

8. When making organizational decisions, relate them to the mission, vision, and philosophy of the organization. Share your decisions and how you made them with your preceptee. Providing care that falls between the competing values of the healthcare organization and the nurse's duty as patient advocate can create obstacles for delivering high quality safe patient care resulting in challenges for maintaining nurse motivation. It may be difficult to challenge authority when a patient situation dictates. Thoughtful mentoring and role modeling provide your preceptee with a positive perspective and strengthens motivation for continuing to provide safe and effective care (Ebright, Carter Kooken, Moody, & Latif Hassan Al-Ishaq, 2006). This strategy demonstrates patient advocacy that is consistent with organizational values, thus minimizing the gap between the two.

9. Recognize your preceptee's accomplishments. Knowing what motivates your preceptee helps you to determine the type of reward or recognition that is valued.

Working with the Experienced Nurse

Autonomy and motivation are closely linked. Researchers found that motivation increased and better outcomes were achieved when learning occurred in a practice setting and when learners were recognized as valued members of the team. As they developed professionally, they earned increasing levels of power, which in turn enhanced their feelings of empowerment. Participation increased proportionately to their motivation to learn (Bradbury-Jones et al., 2007). You may want to incorporate the following strategies to build autonomy in an experienced nurse:

1. Support your preceptee within a nonblaming context. Creating and maintaining an environment where learning can occur even if mistakes happen enhance feelings of competence and facilitate progression.

2. Be approachable. Model this attitude when interacting with coworkers and patients. Approachability suggests an attitude of commitment and that you are there to support your colleagues and patients. Encourage your preceptee to approach you with questions or concerns.

3. Share the organizational structure with your preceptee. Also, share your insight as to who holds formal and informal power within your unit and your organization. Your preceptee will have a clear understanding of the chain of command and will know how to function when engaging authority.

4. Demonstrate high standards for patient advocacy. Practice according to the American Nurses Association Standards of Practice and Code of Ethics.

5. Offer constructive criticism in private. Be prompt and direct but also be supportive and willing to help. This maintains motivation and improves future performance without destroying your preceptee's sense of self.

6. Be enthusiastic. Your preceptee will engage with an equivalent attitude.

7. Be clear when you articulate your expectations for your preceptee's behavior. Knowing what is expected will assist your preceptee to achieve.

Summary

Many preceptor strategies have been presented in this chapter. Review your plan for preceptee progress. Assess your preceptee's level of motivation and implement strategies that help your preceptee achieve. Be enthusiastic and share your enthusiasm. Model a professional practice grounded in ethics and that promotes a high standard of care. Embrace and respect your colleagues, team members, patients, and their families. Be clear, concise, kind, and flexible when interacting with your preceptee. Finally, take time to reflect on what motivates you to stay in nursing. Write out your motivators and keep them in a place that is easily accessible by you. On the days you want to call in sick, review what you have written, get dressed, go to work, and be the best nurse you can be.

Reflection

- Refer to the section in the beginning of this chapter called Questions to Guide Your Learning. After completing this chapter, see if you can answer the questions. Some suggested answers are included in Appendix A.

- The complexities of today's healthcare environment present challenges that may conflict with your internal values and beliefs about nursing. What helps you to maintain your present level of enthusiasm for nursing? How do you maintain motivation to continue your professional nursing career in the future?

- What are your external motivators? What do you believe your preceptee values as external motivators?

- Your preceptee's nursing class has awarded you the honor of presenting the topic "For the Love of Nursing" at their upcoming pinning ceremony. What three pieces of advice will you share with the class that may enhance their love of nursing during difficult times?

- Your preceptee's philosophy of nursing reflects an overall goal to "be the best nurse that I can be." How will you help your preceptee to actualize the goal?

- You assign your preceptee to a patient care task. Your preceptee says, "It is terrible, but I feel incapable of doing the task. Maybe I should go back to school." What do you believe is the cause of your preceptee's reaction? How do you help her?

- You are clearly aware of the complexities of your healthcare environment. How do you create a safe environment for your student preceptee to progress professionally?

- Autonomy is positively linked to retention in nursing. What three strategies do you use to foster an autonomous practice in your experienced nurse preceptee?

References

American Association of Critical Care Nurses. (2005). *Standards for establishing and sustaining healthy work environments: A journey to excellence.* Retrieved February 19, 2008, from http://www.aacn.org/aacn/pubpolcy.nsf/Files/ExecSum/$file/ExecSum.pdf

Ames, C., & Archer, J. (1988). Achievement goals in the classroom: Student's learning strategies and motivation processes. *Journal of Educational Psychology, 80,* 260–267.

Bradbury-Jones, C., Sambrook, S., & Irvine, F. (2007). The meaning of empowerment for nursing students: A critical incident study. *Journal of Advanced Nursing, 59,* 342.

Ebright, P., Carter Kooken, W. S., Moody, R. C., & Latif Hassan Al-Ishaq, M. A. (2006). Mindful attention to complexity: Implications for teaching and learning patient safety. *Annual Review of Nursing Education, 4,* 339–360.

Maslow, A. (1970). *Motivation and personality* (2nd ed.). New York: Harper and Row.

McClelland, D. C. (1971). *Assessing human motivation.* Morristown, NJ: General Learning Press.

Prater, L., & McEwen, M. (2006). Called to nursing: Perceptions of student nurses. *Journal of Holistic Nursing, 24,* 63.

Shunk, D. (1989). Self-efficacy and cognitive skill learning. In C. Ames & R. Ames (Eds.), *Research on motivation in education: goals and cognitions* (Vol. 3, pp. 13–44). San Diego, CA: Academic Press.

NOTES

CHAPTER EIGHT

Bridging Differences: Working with Diversities

> If we are to achieve a richer culture, rich in contrasting values, we must recognize the whole gamut of human potentialities, and so weave a less arbitrary social fabric, one in which each diverse human gift will find a fitting place.
>
> —Margaret Meade

INTRODUCTION

Much attention in the literature has been given to the concept of cultural competence during the past several decades. Nurses are encouraged to demonstrate culturally competent care when interacting with coworkers and with clients within healthcare organizations. But what is it to be culturally competent? And, how is one's success as a culturally competent nurse assessed and measured? Can one achieve cultural competence? More specifically, are you able to provide your culturally diverse preceptee with guidance that is culturally competent? This chapter discusses the limitations of cultural competence as a paradigm. Instead, a simplified version of the journey toward culturally congruent care is presented. Suggestions for how to work with preceptees who are culturally different are explored, and a tool to assess and plan for cultural differences is introduced.

OBJECTIVES

After completing the chapter and related learning activities, you should be able to

1. Differentiate between the terms *culture, cultural competence,* and *cultural congruence.*
2. Identify four organizational artifacts that best represent the espoused culture of your workplace.
3. Identify three artifacts that best define the actual culture of your organization.
4. List four common cultural differences that a preceptor might encounter in a preceptee.

5. Using a simplified model of cultural congruence, develop four preceptor development strategies that demonstrate cultural congruence with your preceptee.

6. Cite two differences between the "Baby Boomer," "X," and "Nexter" generations.

7. Cite three general characteristics of "Baby Boomers." Develop one strategy that could be used when precepting a "Baby Boomer" nurse.

8. Describe two common characteristics of "Nexters." Develop one strategy that may enhance collaboration with a "Nexter" nurse preceptee.

9. Describe three major challenges internationally educated nurses encounter when working outside the borders of their country.

10. Describe three strategies that could be used to manage the challenges described above.

QUESTIONS TO GUIDE YOUR LEARNING

1. What is the difference between culture, cultural competence, and cultural congruence?

2. What are cultural artifacts? Is the culture of your organization reflective of what it is purported to be?

3. Where would organizational artifacts that represent the "real" culture be found?

4. What are four commonly occurring cultural differences?

5. Using the model for developing cultural congruence, what four steps would you take to develop your cultural skills?

6. How do "Baby Boomers," "Generation X," and "Nexters" value the concept of work?

7. What three words would best describe "Baby Boomers"?

8. What is one characteristic that is shared between "Xers" and "Nexters"?

9. What are two of the many challenges that internationally educated nurses experience when first working in the United States?

10. What are three preceptor strategies that might facilitate an internationally educated nurse preceptee's transition into professional practice?

Culture, Cultural Competence, and Cultural Congruence

Culture is the way of life that includes the special beliefs, values, and customs of a particular group of people. Culture is a pattern of behavioral responses that result from imprinting. Over time, social, religious, intellectual, and artistic experiences create similarities of thought. These structures and manifestations, when combined, create culture (Giger and Davidhizar, 2002). Competence is the capacity to function or develop in a particular way and having the necessary skill or knowledge to do something successfully. Therefore in a simple definition, cultural competency is the skill, knowledge, and ability to work in a multicultural environment while being considerate of the customs, beliefs, and values of the particular community, group, or individual. It is a process that is developed over time to increase understanding and gain knowledge of cultural differences that affect, in this case, health care.

There are natural limitations to the paradigm of cultural competence. The study of diversity is limitless because the concept represents all values and beliefs of individuals of all cultures. Cultures are constantly changing and evolving as individuals and groups interact within differing contextual encounters. Values and beliefs develop as a result of these encounters. The United States is heterogeneous and comprises many diverse individuals. To achieve at a culturally competent level, it would be necessary to know and to understand *all* values and beliefs of *all* cultures and diversities embodied by each individual within the context of each encounter, a task that is probably unachievable.

Cultural congruence is another way of thinking about cultural skill development and the application of cultural skill during encounters. To interact with effective tools that are culturally congruent is to recognize that there are cultural differences, sensitivities, and priorities. To demonstrate cultural congruence is to use this knowledge appropriately and safely when engaging in culturally diverse encounters. For the purpose of this chapter, we will be thinking in terms of congruence instead of competence. As an example, as you work with your culturally diverse preceptee, you will recognize that there are differences between you. Your preceptee, who is new to your work group, may be sensitive to nuances in communication between you and your coworkers. To be culturally congruent is to be aware of the difference in communication styles and then share the language of your group with your preceptee so feelings of inclusion are fostered.

Cultural Context

There are many models that illustrate and describe components of cultural skill development, such as those developed by Leininger (1997) and Culhane-Pera, Reif, Egli, Bake, and Kassekert (1997). As a culturally aware preceptor, you've developed interpersonal skills that acknowledge and respect values, beliefs, customs, and the genetic heritage of your preceptee, understanding that these individual components affect how interactions are perceived by the both of you. As you work toward building a trusting relationship with your preceptee, you also develop awareness that trust and respect for differences enhance your encounters and facilitate preceptee role socialization by bridging differences. Cultural congruence does not mean that you must learn everything about each different culture or aspect of diversity but that you develop the skills and resources to interact with and to manage cultural differences. For instance, culturally congruent communication skill development does not suggest learning the primary language of your preceptee, but rather it's gaining the knowledge and skills to communicate effectively within your preceptee's paradigm of life experiences.

It is common to think of cross-cultural differences as being grounded in race and ethnicity. However, study of culture may not be limited to just those differences. Cultural diversity may also include differences such as national origin, age, gender, religion, sexual orientation, mental or physical abilities, social class, and educational level. This chapter focuses on generational and educational diversities, two common diversities you may encounter in your preceptor role.

The cultural framework that defines both you and your preceptee is shaped by life experiences. Additionally, your preceptee–preceptor experiences occur within a context (your work environment) that is secondary but common to the both of you. Therefore cultural congruence becomes a critical skill when interacting not only on a personal or social level but also within a professional context of your healthcare organization's culture. Not only do you need to develop awareness about your preceptee's values and beliefs, but you must also have heightened awareness about how they interface with the culture of your working organization. For instance, the cultural of your organization is that communication between nurses and physicians occurs on a first-name basis. Your preceptee may value social order and communicate using "mister," "misses," or "doctor" when addressing colleagues. This difference in values may be small but may result in cultural misunderstanding.

Assessing Organizational Culture

What is an organization's culture and how is it assessed? Why is it important to understand the culture of the organization for which you work? Knowing the culture of your workplace allows you to assess the employer–employee fit. In your role as preceptor, you help socialize your preceptee into your organization by working with your preceptee to learn about its culture. The organizational culture is the "pattern of shared basic assumptions" that are considered valid enough to share with new members (Schein, 1992). An organization's culture adapts to changes in society, including differences in work force characteristics, such as age and ethnic diversity, and differences in the external environment, such as globalization and competition. Organizational effectiveness is directly proportional to the degree of congruence between an organization, its mission, and the people within the organization. An effective organization generates high revenues as measured financially and by customer satisfaction. The work environment of an effective organization is characterized by maximized quality and quantity of work generated by motivated and satisfied employees. Has your organization changed with the times? Is it a suitable match for new nurses? Let's explore how an organization's culture is assessed.

The first step in assessing organizational culture is to identify relevant artifacts. Artifacts include but are not limited to such things as dress code; the degree of formality found in the organizational hierarchy; decision-making processes; the formal and informal communication networks; and organizational rituals, myths, and stories (Marquis & Huston, 2003). Most organizational artifacts are not retrievable but are learned through observation and through discussions with colleagues. Refer to **Form 8-1** for a guide to assessing the organizational culture.

The second step to knowing and understanding your organization's culture is to compare your observations with those that are explicitly stated. You may compare policy and procedure manuals, marketing materials, the organization's website, and other resources with your observations. Is there congruence between the perceived culture and the actual culture in which you work? Is there harmony between the culture, the mission of the organization, and its people? For example, if your healthcare organization values teaching and learning, as is stated in its mission, does it pay for continuing education? Does the work schedule allow for class attendance? Are promotions considered for those with advanced degrees? If formal education is not valued yet the organization states it believes lifelong learning is integral to its mission, then one might assume there is a lack of congruence between the real value and perceived organizational culture. Completing an organizational cultural assessment helps to determine if the organization is a good fit for your preceptee, resulting in greater job satisfaction and chances for retention. Your preceptee can determine the similarities and differences between personal and organizational values and beliefs. If differences are too great, individual or cultural changes may be necessary to meet cultural standards or to maintain a changing work force.

Developing Cultural Congruence

There are many prescriptions for developing cultural skills that help meet the needs of your preceptee. For an individual or an organization to become culturally congruent, there needs to be a demonstration of a desire to engage in the process. Cultural desire is the willingness and the motivation generated from within yourself, the want and need to know about the way of living of your preceptee. The drive to learn about your preceptee must come from within you and should not be confused with external motivational factors such as regulatory controls that impose standards for action or behavior. Cultural awareness, knowledge, skill, and encounter, when combined with cultural desire, provide skills for working toward culturally congruent interaction (Campinha-Bacote, 2002). Let's examine each of these components more closely.

Cultural Awareness

As you share experiences with your preceptee, you will go through a process of heightened sensitivity to differences between the values, beliefs, and patterns of behavior and life-style practices held by your preceptee and those that you believe and value. Self-analysis and knowledge of *your* values, beliefs, biases, and prejudices should occur for you to anticipate differences you might encounter with your preceptee (Campinha-Bacote, 2002). When both sets of values and beliefs (yours and those of your preceptee) are clearly defined, you are better prepared to guide your preceptee. It is important you consciously avoid imposing your cultural values and beliefs onto your preceptee. During the phase of becoming aware, your challenge is to recognize your biases and stereotypes. As they become increasingly clear, you can be more confident in developing skills that are culturally congruent and that enhance your experiences with your preceptee.

The preceptor strategies presented in this chapter are not differentiated by the level of preceptee experience because cultural diversity is present in both beginner and experienced nurses. The strategies apply to both the new graduate or student and the experienced nurse.

Preceptor Strategies: Cultural Awareness

1. Conduct a self-assessment of your own values, beliefs, and practices (see http://www11.georgetown.edu/research/gucchd/nccc/foundations/assessment.html and www.aafp.org/fpm/20001000/58cult.pdf)

2. Be aware that you will have biases and preconceptions about those who are different from you. These perceptions are usually a product of your past experiences and previous interactions and are frequently based on generalizations. Focus on your preceptee. Communicate. Learn. Validate your perceptions. Becoming more knowledgeable on a personal basis may help you to avoid misconceptions.

3. If left unattended, your biases and preconceptions may impact your relationship with your preceptee. Continue to reflect on and validate or reject your biases.

4. Learn about your preceptee's cultural beliefs and values. Create opportunities for conversations that help you find commonalities between you and your preceptee. Trust will develop as you discover similarities and differences between you.

5. Each person acculturates or socializes differently. Be patient. Your preceptee might integrate into the work environment more quickly or more slowly than other nurses you have precepted or those being precepted by your colleagues.

6. Accept that differing values and beliefs may influence your preceptee's perspective on health and wellness, decision making, illness, and death. Share your perspectives with each other. Work toward understanding the cultural differences.

Cultural Knowledge

Once you are culturally aware, there are things you need to know to develop cultural skills. Cultural knowledge is the process of understanding the values, beliefs, and practices of culturally diverse groups (Campinha-Bacote, 2002). Cultural knowledge may include learning elements of politics, demographics, epidemiology, diet, and socioeconomics. You may learn these things through academics and communication and by actually experiencing different cultures. Read, talk, and experience.

Preceptor Strategies: Cultural Knowledge

1. Establish evidence-based knowledge through reading. Communicate with your preceptee and experience your preceptee's paradigm. Ask questions of your preceptee.

2. Expand your knowledge and exposure to the cultural practices of your preceptee. Validate your findings with your preceptee. You might attend cultural events, go to church, and participate in social outings with your preceptee when appropriate. Celebrate holidays that are not traditional to your culture. Invite your preceptee to do the same.

3. Understand how changes in demographics and sociopolitical influences shape social and personal perspectives of cultural diversity. If your preceptee is from another

country, gain an overall perspective of where your preceptee originated. Learn about the politics, economics, and spiritual history of the country.

4. Appreciate cultural differences. Celebrate and revere the differences between your preceptee and you. Respect these differences and integrate the knowledge into your plan for how you can work effectively with your preceptee.

Developing Culturally Congruent Skills

To interact with cultural congruence requires cultural skill, a term given to the synthesis of empathy, trust, respect, acceptance, communication, and diagnostic skills. These components develop as an outcome of cultural knowledge (Campinha-Bacote, 2002).

Preceptor Strategies: Congruent Skills

1. As your knowledge of culture expands, develop new behavior patterns to meet the needs of your preceptee. Communicate effectively. Convey information in a manner that is clearly understood by your preceptee. If your preceptee speaks English as a second language, communicate in a way that is understandable and respectful. Speak in a manner that is culturally compatible, such as speaking slowly while averting your eyes. Validate your preceptee's understanding of what was being conveyed.

2. Provide supportive written materials so that your preceptee may review content as desired.

3. Provide social support to your preceptee. Understand that he or she is probably feeling isolated. Facilitate integration into your work culture by creating opportunities for interface between coworkers and your preceptee. Suggest ways for your preceptee to become an "insider."

4. Understand that differences between you and your preceptee are neither positive nor negative. They are just different. Work toward acceptance.

Cultural Encounter

Cultural encounter is the experience of cross-cultural interaction (Campinha-Bacote, 2002). Your preceptee–preceptor relationship is based on cross-cultural interactions. Developing awareness, knowledge, and skills prepares you for successful encounters with your preceptee.

Preceptor Strategies: Cultural Encounter

1. You may want to debrief your preceptee at the end of each day or at the conclusion of a complex situation. For instance, if your patient delivers a stillborn infant, you may want to spend some time with your preceptee exploring the events. Reflect on your values about the mother, the infant, and the circumstance. Explore commonalities

and differences in perception and beliefs with your preceptee. Doing so may enhance your relationship and facilitate learning.

2. Be empathetic to your preceptee's needs. Knowing about your preceptee enhances the experiences you share.

3. Reflection is a key element to learning. Use reflection to help you build your repertoire of cultural skills. Analyze encounters to learn your preceptee's values. Compare the similarities and differences between how you and your preceptee think about the experiences. Reflect on encounters. What did you do that enhanced trust, sensitivity, empathy, and respect of another who is culturally or ethnically different? You may want to use **Form 8-2** as you assess and plan for culturally congruent experiences.

Working with Generational and Educational Differences

You may encounter generational and educational differences, in addition to gender and ethnic diversities, in your role as preceptor. Changing work force demographics and globalization of health care contribute to this likelihood. As a preceptor, you may socialize a younger or an older nurse or a nurse who is internationally educated into professional practice. Are you culturally aware? Do you have knowledge and skill to manage encounters with these diversities? As you prepare to assess your preceptee, it is important that differences are not overstated. Yet, at the same time, it is necessary to avoid brushing aside realities. The following is a synopsis of generational characteristics.

Generational Diversity

The literature is rife with much anecdotal information about generational differences. The search engine "Google" produces over 3 million resources when the term "generational differences" is entered. Given the abundance of information, let's review a few of the generational differences you are likely to encounter. Use these generalizations as you would any other. Be aware that the characteristics are representative of many but are not reflective of all individuals. Apply your cultural skills when you assess for your preceptee's generational differences. Validate your assumptions. Learn. Communicate.

Most of your encounters with new nurses will be with those born after 1964. Members of the "X" generation were born between 1964 and 1981. "Nexters" were born between 1981 and 2000 (Clausing, Kurtz, Prendeville, & Walt, 2003).

Generation X

"Generation Xers" believe in a balance between work and life, enjoy flexible time, and are technologically savvy. Generation Xers value and believe in

- Political cynicism
- Challenging traditional roles and values
- Entitlement of rights
- The concept of the primacy of "me"

- Preference for working alone instead of on teams
- Tasks and results
- Diversity in values
- Informality
- Convenience
- The primacy of living over working

Generation X is motivated by a work environment that is balanced with life activities. They seek customization of experiences and appreciate immediate feedback. They embrace flexibility and welcome cross-training and innovation. They like to work in a dynamic environment that is flexible and changeable. They do not require clear lines of authority and appreciate informality in the work place.

Preceptor Strategies: Generation X Nurses

1. Teach your preceptee how to work within a corporate structure. Share the unspoken rules of the organization. Help your preceptee to understand the overall mission of the organization and work with your preceptee to discover how departments, staff, and organizational structure impact each other.

2. Your generation X preceptee is probably comfortable with technology. Use e-mail for follow-up communication. Orient your preceptee to your organization's website. Value your preceptee's entrepreneurial perspective. Encourage your preceptee's contribution to the organization.

3. Use informal communication techniques. Talk in short sentences. Seek your preceptee's feedback. Validate or verify your preceptee's understanding.

4. Assume that your preceptee is intelligent and ambitious. Create opportunities for your preceptee to participate in projects. Empower your preceptee to make decisions.

5. Teach your preceptee new skills. Use collaboration as you help to build your preceptee's plan of professional progression.

6. Give your preceptee frequent feedback and recognition. Evaluate your preceptee using accurate, specific, and timely feedback.

7. Value your preceptee's commitment to maintaining the balance between work and personal life. Maintain flexibility in planning experiences.

The "Nexter" Generation

"Nexters" include people born between 1981 and 2000. They are generally concerned about trying to clean up that which was left to them by previous generations. As a result, they have a strong sense of civic duty. They are knowledgeable and are tolerant of diversity. They typically value their lifestyle above work. Nexters enjoy humor and prefer to work in a fun environment that allows for time off and flexible scheduling. Nexters are goal oriented. They need little assistance defining goals and require limited guidance in meeting them. They want to be involved and thrive in creative and collaborative interactions. Nexters enjoy the social benefits of mentorship, but learning strategies must be designed that are short in duration and intensive in style. Nexters value and believe in

- Self-confidence
- Lifestyle over work
- Action and achievement
- Reside with their parents
- Education, sports, and fitness
- Are responsible and have a strong sense of work ethic
- Collaboration

Preceptor Strategies: Nexter Nurses

1. Plan strategies that maintain attention, because Nexters are fast movers.
2. Use action words that challenge your preceptee toward goal achievement.
3. Structure is important to the Nexter preceptee. Providing structure helps your preceptee to focus on goals.
4. Seek your preceptee's feedback. Nexters hold few biases and generally appreciate diversity that results in honest and open dialogue.
5. Appreciate your preceptee's level of self-confidence. Encourage informed risk-taking behavior (structure). Help your preceptee to plan for the results of decisions.
6. Your preceptee may question your authority or seek clarification from others. Seek to understand that your preceptee believes there is more than one answer to a question. Appreciate that your preceptee will ask many questions. Help your Nexter preceptee learn to interact with others. Goal achievement, ability to multitask, and a belief that it is a social responsibility to question authority may create challenges with interpersonal interactions.
7. Provide opportunities for collaboration. Keep your preceptee challenged with projects and meaningful work. Allow your preceptee's input on how to do a task.

The Baby Boomer Generation

Organizations are turning to creative retention and recruitment strategies to meet staffing needs. Administrators are calling on retired nurses and internationally educated nurses (IENs) to fill vacant positions. As a member of Generation X or as a Nexter, do you demonstrate a culturally congruent skill set to help you precept a nurse older than you? What do you need to know to enhance your role as a preceptor?

Chances are that an "older" nurse called into practice from retirement is a "Baby Boomer." It is important to know that experienced nurses returning to practice from retirement have wisdom and experiences to share. Baby Boomers value and believe in

- Taking control of situations
- Being in a leadership role
- Peacefulness and generally avoiding conflict
- In the primacy of self and seek to change much of what surrounds them
- Strong work ethic, which is why they are termed "workaholics"
- Recognition for hard work and commitment

Preceptor Strategies: Baby Boomer Nurses

- Encourage self-direction.
- Allow your preceptee to take the lead when establishing goals.
- Enhance understanding and avoid conflict by answering questions completely. Provide many details.
- Help your preceptee to develop conflict management skills.
- To avoid burnout, help your preceptee set appropriate limits. Because Baby Boomers are enthusiastic about work, they may "take on" more than is required.
- Use traditional rewards when recognizing your preceptee's hard work. A well-written "thank you" goes a long way with Baby Boomers.
- Use books and training materials to support your preceptee. Allow for opportunities for end-of-day discussions that generate analyses.

Educational Diversity: The Internationally Educated Nurse

This workbook presents a great deal of material to help you to understand and to work with differences in educational preparation and experience. You know how to work with beginners and with experienced nurses. You've been presented with strategies to help you develop skills in managing cross-cultural encounters. However, knowing these things is not enough.

Healthcare organizations have expanded their recruitment strategies to include international nurses. Although IENs earn their professional license as registered nurses by successfully completing the National Council Licensing Examination-Registered Nurse (i.e., NCLEX-RN) examination, the context of their professional practice may be vastly different from those in the United States, which can create challenges for successful socialization.

Challenges Facing IENs Practicing in the United States

Data indicate that most IENs fall between the ages of 23 and 32, with 15% being male (Davis & Nichols, 2002). Philippine nursing education programs provide nursing education at the baccalaureate level. Most Canadian provinces require the baccalaureate for entry into practice. India, South Africa, and Nigeria support both baccalaureate and diploma programs, with most nurses being educated at the diploma level. Of the top five countries for foreign recruitment, all present nursing education in English, yet a small fraction of the Commission on Graduates of Foreign Nursing Schools test-takers cite English as their primary language (Davis & Nichols, 2002).

In 1999 and 2000 the Commission on Graduates of Foreign Nursing Schools compiled data elicited from focus groups conducted throughout the United States and found that language, culture, and the practice of nursing were predominant challenges for IENs practicing outside their countries of origin (Davis & Nichols, 2002).

Even though their nursing education was presented in English, most IENs cite another language as their primary language of communication. However, misunderstandings and misinterpretations occur because the language of our culture is replete with idiomatic expressions that are frequently lost on nurses speaking English as their second language. Lack of cultural knowledge can reflect an unintentional lack of sensitivity, resulting in misperceptions.

The challenge becomes more complex when the nondominant culture of the IEN intersects with the culture of the organization in which they're practicing in the United States. These two cultures (the IEN's and the organization's) interact, and variations in values and beliefs can create an opportunity for misunderstanding.

IENs frequently do not understand the language of U.S. health care. Most IENs originate from countries that do not have health insurance and are not familiar with the threads that weave the language of insurance-supported care. "Preferred provider," "health maintenance organizations," and "copayment" are uncommon concepts in countries outside the United States. The names of medical tests, blood panels, and racially related diseases are abundant. An IEN from Sri Lanka may have no knowledge of sickle cell anemia, just as a nurse from the United States may have no exposure to a patient diagnosed with River Blindness.

Even though IENs are language proficient, challenges with interpersonal relationships may result because of differences in cultural awareness and knowledge. In the United States, many people are accustomed to maintaining eye contact and giving nonverbal feedback by leaning forward, smiling, and nodding. Certain behaviors such as prolonged eye contact, erect posture, looking down on someone with lowered lids, hands on hips, or holding the head high may be interpreted as assertive or aggressive. People from other backgrounds may show respect or deference by avoiding eye contact and communicate using passive body language. It could be misconstrued that if a nurse does not demonstrate assertiveness, ask questions, and advocate for patients, the nurse is providing less than stellar patient advocacy skills. However, some cultures are paternalistic, and nurses are expected to follow physician orders without question—assertiveness is not a role expectation.

Alienation and prejudice contribute to IEN feelings of isolation. When in her or his own country, the nurse is in the cultural majority. When practicing abroad, the IEN is a member of the minority and can suffer exposure to prejudice from uninformed patients, coworkers, and administration.

Acculturation is an intense time of stress and learning. Activities of daily living, sense of home and family, and the context of her or his professional practice are all areas in which IENs can experience stress. The IEN's family paradigm changes as most nurses arrive in the

United States with their families to follow. The routine of the day is different, and activities of daily living that were once automatic require a great deal of thought and planning. Sources of food, housing, transportation, and social support are new and different. The context of her professional practice is different and requires adaptation to perhaps a different scope of practice, care standards, and work practices.

Cultural Congruence: The IEN

IENs may be more challenging to work with from a perspective of cultural congruence. The cultural assimilation for an IEN may be multifaceted. Your preceptee may need help to transition into the role of a U.S. nurse and the role of a member of a new community in a "foreign" country. The IEN preceptee may be challenged in communication and managing life skills and may be of a different generation. In thinking about this you may throw up your hands. Do so not in frustration but in excitement. Embrace the journey you are preparing to take by reading, communicating, and experiencing.

Preceptor Strategies: Working With IENs

1. Be *aware* of cultural differences between you and your preceptee.

2. Analyze your preconceived notions about your preceptee.

3. Validate or reject your perceptions by reading relevant material about your preceptee's differences. Communicate with your preceptee. Share stories and in doing so discover your similarities and differences.

4. *Know* about the country from which your preceptee originated. Learn its political, economic, and social structures. Read about local customs. Validate your findings with your preceptee. Experience your preceptee's spiritual paradigm. Celebrate holidays that are valued by both you and your preceptee. As you learn about differences, you will also learn similarities.

5. Develop *congruent skills* that promote trust, respect, and value. Be empathetic with your preceptee. Congruent skills develop proportionately to increased knowledge. The more you know, the more you care. Honor your preceptee's beliefs.

6. Support your preceptee's *encounters*. Your IEN preceptee is learning on many different levels. Every interaction is an encounter in which both you and your preceptee have the opportunity to learn. Explain situations and validate perceptions.

7. *Reflect* on your encounters. Collaboratively review the outcomes. Share strategies for improvement and celebrate successes.

Summary

Wow! This is exciting. Not only are you the teacher, you are also going to learn something new each day you experience a culture encounter. A cultural encounter is any interaction you have with another. During that exchange, you have an opportunity to anticipate differences, learn about them, and develop skills that meet both your needs and the needs of the diverse preceptee. Read, communicate, experience, and reflect your way to cultural congruence.

Reflection

- Refer to the section in the beginning of this chapter called Questions to Guide Your Learning. After completing this chapter, see if you can answer the questions. Some suggested answers are included in Appendix A.

- What culturally congruent skills have you developed to help you as a preceptor?

- What are the cultural differences between you and your preceptee? How can you provide for culturally congruent encounters with your preceptee?

- Describe the culture of your organization. Does it support education? Are you given a more challenging patient care assignment because you are precepting a new nurse? Does your organization promote cultural competence through internal programming or classes? Is attendance in such a program required by all employees of your organization?

- Do you have a preconception about the outcome of your preceptee–preceptor experience? On what is it based?

- Do you believe there are value differences between a 60-year-old nurse and a 23-year-old nurse? If so, what are some of the differences? What are the similarities? From which experiences do you draw your conclusions?

- What three things would you do to facilitate your 58-year-old preceptee's reintroduction into practice?

- You are 56 years old. What are some of the challenges you might encounter when precepting a Nexter?

- Do you have a preconception about your 24-year-old preceptee who still resides at the parental home?

- Do you have any preconceptions about IENs? What are they? How will you validate them?

- Have you ever precepted or worked with an IEN? What did you do to make the encounter successful?

References

Campinha-Bacote, J. (2002). The process of cultural competence in the delivery of healthcare services: A model of care. *Journal of Transcultural Nursing, 13*(3), 181–184.

Clausing, S. L., Kurtz, D. L., Prendeville, J., & Walt, J. L. (2003). Generational diversity—the Nexters. *AORN Journal, 78,* 373.

Culhane-Pera, K. A., Reif, C., Egli, E., Bake, N. J., & Kassekert, R. A. (1997). Curriculum for multicultural education in family medicine. *Family Medicine, 29,* 719–723.

Davis, C., & Nichols, B. (2002). Foreign-educated nurses and the changing U.S. nursing workforce. *Nursing Administration Quarterly, 26,* 43–51.

Giger, J., & Davidhizar, R. E. (2002). The Giger and Davidhizar transcultural assessment model. *Journal of Transcultural Nursing, 13*(3), 185–188.

Newman. J., Davidhizar, R. E., & Fordham, P. (2006). Multi-cultural and multi-ethnic considerations and advanced directives: Developing cultural competency. *Journal of Cultural Diversity, 13,* 3–9.

Leininger, M. (1997). Transcultural nursing: A scientific and humanistic discipline. *Journal of Transcultural Nursing, 8,* 54–55.

Marquis, B. L., & Huston, C. L. (2003). *Leadership roles and management functions in nursing theory and application* (4th ed). Philadelphia: Lippincott Williams & Wilkins.

Schein, E. (1992). *Organizational culture and leadership* (2nd ed.). San Francisco: Jossey-Bass.

NOTES

FORM 8-1: ORGANIZATIONAL CULTURAL ASSESSMENT TOOL

Facilitate your preceptee's acculturation into your organization by gathering the following data:

Artifacts	Question	Observations	Congruent Between Actual and Exposed
Physical	Is the work environment attractive? Is the environment well maintained? Is the lobby appropriate in size? Is it well lit? Is it organized? Is the nursing station quiet? Roomy? Organized? Are there conference rooms? Are there quiet places for families to convene?		
Social	Do work colleagues maintain friendships outside the organization? Are there organizational activities that are well attended by employees? Picnics? Bowling teams? Holiday parties? Do employees appear to like each other? How do departments get along with each other? What is the level of formality within relationships? Are first names used between nurses? When speaking with physicians? With supervisors? Is humor found within the organization? Are security guards present? Is employee parking well lighted? Are escorts available? How does one become a member of "the group"?		
Organizational	What are the working hours? Is promptness expected? What is the dress code? Is it different per unit?		

(continues)

FORM 8-1: ORGANIZATIONAL CULTURAL ASSESSMENT TOOL (CONTINUED)

Artifacts	Question	Observations	Congruent Between Actual and Exposed
	How are decisions made? How do you lean things about the organization?		
	Are there frequent meetings? Are they prescheduled? Are they on time? How are they run?		
	Is there local jargon used? Are there different symbols of identity?		
	What are the rites and rituals of the organization?		
	Is family valued? Is there balance between work and family?		
	What are the espoused values of the organization? What are the actual values of the organization? Are there differences between the two?		
	Is education rewarded? Is there a tuition reimbursement program? Is paid time off awarded to those continuing their education?		

FORM 8-2: CULTURAL ASSESSMENT OF YOUR PRECEPTEE

Use the form to help you to plan how you will work with your preceptee using culturally congruent skills.

Cultural Awareness List potential differences	Cultural Knowledge List things you need to know about each of the differences	Cultural Skills Identify the skills you need to implement knowledge	Cultural Encounter List opportunities for skill implementation	Reflection Describe outcomes Create a plan for improvement Describe celebration of success

CHAPTER NINE

Assessing Preceptee Progress: How Are We Doing?

One ship sails east, and another west, by the self-same winds that blow, 'tis the set of the sails and not the gales, that tells the way we go.

—Ella Wheeler Wilcox

INTRODUCTION

If you are going to take the extra time and effort to precept a new employee, you want to come to the end of the experience with a "keeper," someone you want to work with as a fellow professional. As the quote above suggests, to make that happen you need to know where you want to get to. Assessing to be sure you are going in the right direction (developing a "keeper") involves knowing where you want to get to by setting performance goals and objectives, looking at performance, and making decisions about how well goals and objectives are being achieved.

The purpose of this chapter is to help you with the process of continuously assessing your preceptee so it becomes a positive activity that leads to positive changes toward desired goals and objectives. You will be assessing preceptee developing knowledge and capabilities. The preceptee should also be assessing progress as well as the process of how the two of you are working together. The chapter includes descriptions of assessment processes or approaches and several useful assessment tools.

OBJECTIVES

After completing the chapter and related learning activities, you should be able to

1. Differentiate the focus of assessment and evaluation.
2. Describe preceptor roles in the four processes of continuous assessment.
3. Differentiate (describe) goals and objectives.

4. Write goals and objectives for your preceptee's learning outcomes for both periodic and end of precepted experience.

5. Use goals and objectives to guide decisions about preceptee progress.

6. Describe appropriate timing for giving preceptee feedback about performance.

7. Describe appropriate use of assessment tools: anecdotal notes, checklist, journals, conferences, questioning, and role play.

8. Involve all stakeholders in determining expected outcomes and assessment of outcomes.

9. Describe the components of an effective objective.

10. Given examples of objectives, select components of an effective objective.

11. Describe (write) objectives that include components of an effective objective.

12. Use positive collaborative approaches (focused on desired changes rather than negative behaviors) to monitor and improve preceptee's progression (defined expected outcomes).

13. Given examples of preceptor facilitating behaviors and nonfacilitating behaviors, accurately chooses (circles) those that facilitate and those that do not.

14. Use established goals and objectives to involve the preceptee in self-assessment during daily, weekly, and precepted time frames.

15. Use established preceptor roles and expectations to involve the preceptee in assessing the preceptor's achievement.

16. Describe the preceptor role in final evaluation of the preceptee.

QUESTIONS TO GUIDE YOUR LEARNING:

1. What is the difference between assessment and evaluation?

2. What will you assess about your preceptee?

3. What are four processes used in assessing performance? How should your preceptee be involved in these processes?

4. In what way should you use objectives when assessing your preceptee's performance?

5. What is the best timing for giving performance feedback? What is the purpose of providing for feedback about the preceptee's performance?

6. How might stakeholders influence the assessment process? How can you involve them in the process?

7. What are the differences between goals and objectives?

8. What do objectives describe?

9. What are three components of useful objectives?

10. What should the observable behavior component of an objective describe?

11. What are factors that could be described in expected standards?

12. What are three recommendations for facilitating psychomotor skill development?

13. Who should be involved in planning for achieving objectives?

14. What are examples of preceptor behaviors that interfere with preceptee learning?

15. How would you tell your preceptee that something he or she has done does not meet expectations?

16. How will your teaching vary because of your preceptee's learning style?

17. How will you involve your preceptee in self-assessment? In assessing your precepting behaviors?

18. How would you react in the following situations?

   • You note that one of your preceptee's patients is more acutely ill than the others and you have discussed this with the preceptee. You see that the preceptee has checked medications and is assessing other patients before going into the sicker patient's room.

   • Your preceptee is giving a very disorganized patient report. The preceptee leaves out quite a few vital points and keeps looking through her notes to find report items so report lasts a long time.

   • Your preceptee is not a self-starter. She waits for you to tell her to try a new procedure. You would like her to jump in and offer to do this on her own, without your prompting or pushing her to get the experience.

   • A patient tells you that the preceptee makes her nervous. The patient says the preceptee doesn't seem to know how to operate the intravenous pump.

19. Which of the following sample learning objectives contains all the elements of effective objectives (add characteristics that make the objective effective if it is lacking one or more elements)?

   • Understands two purposes of writing anecdotal notes in assessing skill progression.

   • Given the assignment of four patients, accurately lists in priority order the degree to which those patients are in jeopardy of rapidly becoming more critically ill.

   • Knows the rationale for checking gastric residual in patients being fed via nasogastric tube.

   • Given three Chem-6 laboratory results, selects (verbally) those results that are in the abnormal range without error.

Assessment Process

Some assessment literature uses assessment and evaluation as if the terms were synonymous. Other sources argue there is a distinct difference. Whereas assessment involves looking for learning gains (what the learner knows and is able to do), evaluation involves making judgments about what was observed or measured (Bastable, 2003; Zvacek, 1999). For our purposes assessment includes both processes: observation for intended outcomes and judgment about the qualities of what was observed.

Let's take a look at the process of assessment. In the precepted setting the type of assessment you are involved in is performance assessment or authentic assessment (Palomba & Banta, 1999). What the preceptee knows and is able to do will be revealed in his or her performance. You will be accumulating information about performances you observe as you are working with the preceptee. **Figure 9-1** shows the four processes involved in assessment. Each process is described as well as some specific strategies for carrying out assessment of your preceptee.

Developing Clear Goals and Objectives: Setting Your Sails

The starting place for assessment is to know and describe what you want the preceptee to know and be able to do, the outcome behaviors you want to observe in your preceptee. It is vital that you define goals and objectives for the preceptee's experiences. These goals and objectives need to be clear, specific, observable, and communicated to the preceptee and other stakeholders.

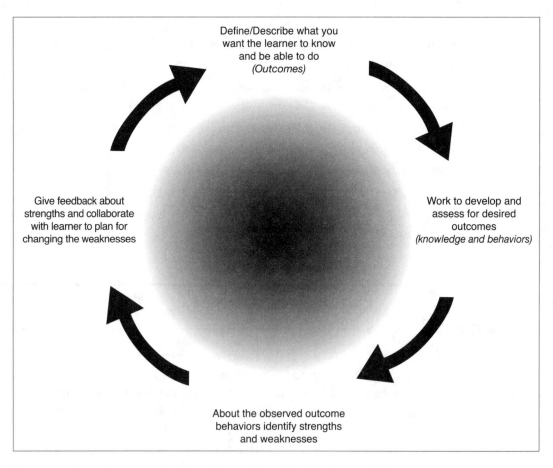

Figure 9-1. Component processes of assessing and improving learning outcomes.

Observing and Measuring for Desired Objectives or Outcomes

Once the expectations are identified for daily, weekly, monthly, and final outcomes, you and your preceptee need to develop and implement strategies for achieving the outcomes and then observe for expected performances frequently during the precepted experiences. This should be done not only at the end of the experience but throughout the experience. The preceptor should observe the preceptee's performance; however, the preceptee should also be encouraged and assisted in looking at his or her own behaviors.

Making Judgments About Observations

After observing preceptee performances, you and the preceptee should work together to identify strengths and weaknesses in the performances you have observed. Ask the preceptee to describe what he or she thought of the day's performance or of a specific incident. You should also share your impressions of performance.

Working to Improve Behaviors

Assessment should provide opportunities for correcting or improving behaviors as well as continuing and strengthening positive behaviors; therefore the sooner you give feedback about performance, the more time available for correcting and building behaviors. Work with your preceptee to plan for ways of improving behaviors.

You may feel sorry for your preceptee or be uncomfortable discussing weaknesses. You may be so uncomfortable that you inflate your evaluation of performance. Consider the potential consequences. The behavior will continue and possibly worsen. You may ultimately not be able to retain the preceptee or give a good evaluation to a faculty person, leading to an unnecessary student failure. On the other hand, had you dealt with the problem in a constructive facilitative way earlier in the experience, you may have helped the preceptee develop more favorably. Please don't ignore or shy away from correcting unacceptable preceptee behaviors, and don't inflate your evaluations!

General Preceptor Assessment Strategies

Think about strategies you may want to use so that you are continuously working to improve behaviors. These would include such factors as knowing and interacting with all stakeholders in assessing the preceptee, writing objectives, devising ways to collaboratively plan for achieving these objectives, finding effective ways to develop psychomotor skills, using facilitating communication, encouraging self-evaluation and reflection, and considering your preceptee's learning styles or preferences. Each of these is described in more detail.

Including All Stakeholders

Stakeholders may be involved in providing information about preceptee outcomes. They may also have responsibilities for assessing the preceptee. They may be involved in accepting or rejecting the preceptee. They may disapprove or resent the time you spend with the preceptee.

You need to know who will be involved in the assessment process and who will make final evaluative decisions about assessments. Will a faculty member be involved or have the total responsibility? How will the unit manager be involved? If the preceptee is a new employee, how do the education and human resources departments become involved, if at all? How are other staff members on your unit involved? It is important to involve all stakeholders who are going to be making decisions based on your assessments. In one hospital where we placed students with preceptors, all the staff on the unit made final decisions about their potential coworker. If this is the case on your unit, you probably want to involve him or her in determining goals and objectives, or at least get his or her agreement with them. It is also important to involve them in periodic assessments of the preceptee's progression, which allows the preceptee's performance to be modified and improved. What a waste it would be if, at the end of the precepted time, the staff did not want to retain the preceptee because you didn't involve them in the assessment process. You thought the preceptee's performance was acceptable but the staff did not. There was, therefore, no opportunity to facilitate preceptee changes so the staff would approve retention.

It is important to include stakeholders in either developing or approving the intended outcomes of the experience. They should also be involved in making decisions about any changes in how you work with the team. Involve them in periodic summaries of preceptee progress. Ask for their observations of preceptee performance. If they are involved in evaluating the preceptee, share your observations and judgments about performance periodically before the end of the experience.

Using Continuous Interactive Processes

Use assessment tools every time you work with your preceptee. Don't wait to discuss something you or the preceptee has observed. Discuss it as close to the observation as possible. This way you and the preceptee can continuously work to strengthen behaviors. Addressing it immediately increases the time available for positive changes.

Be sure you involve the preceptee in self-evaluation. Doing this consistently helps to develop a habit of reflection and facilitates the preceptee's becoming increasingly self-directed and motivated.

Developing Goals and Objectives

You and the preceptee need to clearly define benchmarks for achievement throughout the precepted experience. Establish daily, weekly, and monthly benchmarks. Develop clear goals and objectives so you can validate that appropriate knowledge and behaviors are being developed.

There may be some predefined expected outcomes in your agency such as the policies and procedures used for performance evaluation of nurses. If you're precepting students, expected outcomes may also come from a school of nursing. In this case the school will communicate performance expectations. Another source of outcome descriptions is the policy and procedure manual in your agency and on your unit, if there are procedures specific to your unit. Both agency and the school of nursing expectations will tend to be outcomes that should be apparent at the *end* of the experience. You also need to set goals and objectives that facilitate progress toward those final outcomes. Generally, these are developed by you and the preceptee and possibly other stakeholders.

Not only will you assess the preceptee, but the preceptee should be assessing and evaluating the precepted experiences and your performance as a preceptor. If your agency doesn't have developed assessment forms, you may want to use or modify the forms at the end of this chapter (see **Form 9-1, Form 9-2,** and **Form 9-3**).

Differentiating Goals and Objectives

Goals tend to be global, whereas objectives need to be specific and more focused on steps that achieve the more global goals. An example of a goal might be, "At the end of the precepted experiences the preceptee will demonstrate behavior that exemplifies the ANA scope and standards of practice." Objectives would then need to describe how the preceptee will develop these practices and how well they should be developed.

Developing Clear Objectives

Clearly developed objectives help you and the preceptee select experiences that achieve the desired knowledge and behaviors. They help guide the way to improving performance. They offer a view of the value of expected performances which is very important for adult learners. Knowing the importance of learning something helps to motivate learning. Objectives describe

- What you want the preceptee to know and be able to do.

- Outcomes, not processes used to get to the outcomes. For example, they would describe "Safely and accurately prepares and administers medications to five patients, within plus or minus 30 minutes of ordered time, without error." They would *not* describe, "Increase number of assigned patients from two to five, including medication administration." This would be a process rather than an outcome.

- Specific, observable, measurable behaviors rather than broad, intangible, or unobservable behaviors, like "understands" or "knows" or "appreciates." Even though you want the learner to know something, you cannot observe knowing. You need to describe a behavior that would specify or reveal that the learner knew what you wanted him or her to know.

- Student knowledge and behaviors, not teacher behaviors. For example, "Encourage preceptee to write a list of . . ." describes your behavior, not the preceptee's outcome behaviors that would result from listing.

Objectives should describe three components: observable behavior, any provisions or specifications under which the behavior should occur (if any), and standards by which the behavior will be judged (or how well you want the learner to perform the behavior) (Mager, 1997).

- Observable behavior
  - Describe *something the preceptee will be doing*, something you can observe that indicates what the preceptee knows or is able to do.
  - The behavior must be something you can *observe*. If the behavior cannot be observed, describe an observable behavior that specifies or reveals what the learner knew or was able to do. For example, instead of "Knows correct procedure for _____" (can't observe knows), say, "Uses appropriate steps as described in procedure manual to complete a _____" (using procedure steps is the specified behavior). Instead of "Understands principles (which can't be observed) of preventing bloodborne infection," say "Consistently applies universal precautions when ___" (Universal precautions are specifically spelled out in the agency's policies and procedures and they can be observed).
  - The behavior should describe the *key or most important* desired behavior. An example of an objective that does *not* describe the key desired behavior is, "Given lists of four meals, can circle the one that provides the highest sodium." Circling is *not* the key desired behavior. The key behavior is that the learner is able to select foods with high sodium content. The learner does this by circling the correct answer, "Given lists of foods in four meals, identifies (circles) foods with high sodium content." You can't observe "identifies" but you can see the behavior, "circling," that reveals this ability.
- Provisions, limitations, or requirements (if any) under which the preceptee will be performing the intended behavior.
  - For example, you might say "Given three patients with renal insufficiency, is able to ___." Or, "Using a conversion table, writes the correct drip rate for ___." Note: There may be *no* specified provisions, limitations, or requirements. This is not a crucial component of useful objectives if there are no imposed circumstances.
- Expected standards
  - It is important to describe *how well* you want the preceptee to perform a behavior. Standards might include components of speed, accuracy, quantity, qualities, or critical required behaviors. Examples of a standard might be, "Demonstrates ___ achieving all of the steps (*standard*) described in the critical requirements checklist." Anther example might be, "Names 3 of the possible 5 _____" (*standard*). Note: Ensure that it is safe for the preceptee to know only three. Instead, you might want to

say, "Names all 5 of the triggers for _____ without error" (*standard*). Review **Form 9-4** with your preceptee when you develop objectives.

Facilitating Psychomotor Skill Development

Your preceptee has developed some degree of skill in performing commonly recurring skills; however, there is a need to practice those skills to improve speed, flexibility, and automatic performance. Your preceptee builds psychomotor skills in day-to-day experiences with you. It is important that you facilitate preceptee skill performance in assessing patients, maintaining and operating equipment, and administering medications and treatments.

Psychomotor skill development progresses through stages (Simpson, 1972). Skills develop through conscious effort, relatively slowly, step-by-step, following directions or copying observed steps, through developing increasing speed, accuracy, and flexibility to being able to perform the skill rapidly, smoothly, and automatically, without much conscious effort. Skills develop through these stages as the learner has opportunities to practice them.

When facilitating skill progression, consider the complexity of the skill and how frequently the preceptee may have opportunities to practice the skill. Skill progression occurs more rapidly and with less help when the task is simple and predictable. If the skill is more complex and how one performs the procedure depends on patient responses or other environmental factors that require decision making to change or modify the procedure, then the skill will develop more slowly (Romiszowski, 1999).

Recommendations for facilitating psychomotor skill development when the skill is new or infrequently encountered include the following (Bastable, 2003; Romiszowski, 1999):

- Provide or make accessible any needed background information before practicing or demonstrating a procedure.

- Provide a model of the skill, for example, written step-by-step instruction, a video, or real-time demonstration. Provide a sequential demonstration of the whole skill, or mentally review the procedure if the learner has had previous limited experiences. Be sure to demonstrate from the performer's viewpoint. For example, stand next to the learner rather than across from the learner so the task is upside down or backward in the learner's perception.

- If the task is quite complex, needing several smaller sets of tasks, it is better to break it down into sets of component tasks and teach one set of tasks and let the learner develop skill in that first set, and then teach the second set of steps and allow for skill development of those tasks. After skill is developed in the first and second set, have the learner practice both first and second set together. Proceed through remaining task sets in the same manner, putting together all sets after they are learned individually.

- After demonstrating the steps of a new skill, have the preceptee perform the skill. During the preceptee's first one or two performances, offer verbal guidance to provide information to the preceptee about the procedure performance.

- When the preceptee has developed some skill in a procedure, do not interrupt performance to give guidance or feedback unless harm might occur. Discuss the performance and ask questions about rationale or theoretical applications before or after the performance, not during the performance. Let the learner fully concentrate on the procedure.

- Encourage mental review or rehearsal of the procedure steps.

- When possible, supply verbal cueing of the procedure steps. An example of this is "ABC" cues of airway, breathing, and circulation when encountering an unconscious person.

- Provide opportunities for practice.

- Remember to give or provide for feedback. Reflecting about results of actions and debriefing about performance behaviors improves learning (Gaberson & Oermann, 2007).

Planning for Achieving Objectives

Again, it is essential to include all stakeholders as appropriate for your situation. It would be counterproductive to plan how you and the preceptor will proceed if some stakeholders would not approve or allow that process.

You and the preceptee should plan activities that achieve goals and objectives. Make plans to gradually add activities. Add activities that progressively increase in complexity or difficulty. For example, taking into account the preceptee's past experience, plan to start with procedures or skills that are not too difficult and that the preceptee has some but not sufficient experience, and then move to those with which the preceptee has had little or no experience and that are increasingly difficult. Remember to use your preceptee's experiences rather than your *own* experiences. Some examples of factors that influence complexity are number of patients and their families; patients' diagnoses; number of medications; number and difficulty of procedures; predictability of patient's response to illness and therapy; unstable, emergent, or changing problems; and need for coordinating with others.

Be sure to include skill development plans for all common procedures and diagnoses occurring on your unit. You may want to use a written form of tracking. It is helpful to write a plan for the entire experience and then plan for monthly and weekly progression. Daily planning should lay out ways of achieving the week's plan and so on. **Form 9-5, Form 9-6,** and **Form 9-7** are sample tracking forms. You may want to involve your preceptee in developing modifications to these forms. You may also want to refer to the forms in Chapters 1 and 3.

Using Facilitative Approaches

Use facilitating, supportive, encouraging behaviors while working with your preceptee. Think of your role as a coach, advisor, guide, and resource facilitator rather than a supervisor or critic. Nonfacilitating preceptor behaviors can interfere with or slow preceptee learning. These behaviors obstruct professional growth and preceptee confidence. Examples of nonfacilitating behaviors include being unavailable for conferencing, assistance, or advice when needed; placing in situations for which the preceptee has no preparation or would have difficulty managing; over supervising or under supervising; belittling the preceptee or criticizing in front of others; or withholding information to see if the preceptee notices a problem.

Using positive facilitating approaches, you should provide for continuous feedback to your preceptee. You should work to keep your approaches and communication constructive and as objective as possible. For example, try to objectively describe what you observe, without negative judgmental interpretations, and to offer suggestions about what should be done rather than what should not be done (Gaberson & Oermann, 2007). For example, in giving feedback or discussing a situation, you might say, "When Mr. James started bleeding, I noticed that you went into his room, then came right back out. You went into the linen room, then into the medication area. It didn't seem as if you took definite action for awhile. What was going on in your mind?" You might also add: "Let's take a look at what you would do differently if this were to happen again?" You would not want to give it a negative slant by saying, "When Mr. James started bleeding, you should not have ..." The latter approach is negative. It tells the preceptee what *not* to do rather than what *to do*. The preceptee would gain knowledge about what not to do, but you did not help to develop an acceptable response. It also doesn't give the preceptee a chance to develop habits of problem-solving responses. When you need to do something corrective with your preceptee, you might want to think through a positive way of correcting the behavior before taking action.

Build trust with your preceptee so that feelings of safety and confidence develop. The preceptee will anticipate that you will choose situations that require skills the preceptee is able to perform. The preceptee should feel that it is safe to engage in critical reflection. This is more likely to occur if you avoid negative behaviors described above, if you carefully plan for appropriate development, progressively adding skills, and if you encourage the preceptee to be reflective and to engage in self-evaluation and planning for improvement.

Considering the Preceptee's Learning Styles

In Chapter 6 you learned about adult learning and ways of working with adult learners. You also learned about differing learning styles, that people have preferred ways of taking in and processing information. You also explored a variety of teaching–learning strategies that appealed to differing learning preferences. Remember that your style may be very different from your preceptee. You may want to try differing approaches that seem to help your preceptee grasp and process information. Refer back to Chapter 6 for more strategies you might try. Include your preceptee in this as well.

Encouraging Self-Evaluation and Goal Planning

Self-evaluation and self-direction facilitates progress in skill development. Reflecting about experiences and determining ways of positively changing behaviors or strengthening behaviors enhances the ability to recall events and apply what was learned in a similar situation.

Being self-directed also boosts the preceptee's self-confidence. Telling the preceptee how to change or improve (which may at times be a good approach but should not be the predominant approach) communicates that you may not trust that person's ability to perform on his or her own. It does not build a habit of analyzing situations and making sound decisions. Instead, it builds a habit of dependency.

Assessment Tools

How do you proceed to use these assessment processes? Several assessment tools you can use to gather information about your preceptee's progression are described below. You can choose those you believe will work for you and for the situation.

Observation

Periodically observe how your preceptee is performing. Be as objective as you can so that you note behavior specifics rather than immediately passing judgment on them. Be sure to clarify and verify your perceptions with the preceptee to be sure your observations about performance are accurate.

Anecdotal Notes

As you observe your preceptee's behavior, you may want to take some notes so that you can later reflect about the behaviors, see trends, and share observations with your preceptee. You may notice something that troubles you a bit but decide to wait to see if the behavior occurs again before sharing your observations because the situation was somewhat unusual. The anecdotal note may include descriptions of performances you observed and any judgments you made about the behaviors. Write about your observations as soon after you saw them and share them with your preceptee as soon as possible (Gronlund, 2006). Be sure to focus your observations on the goals and objectives you established. You are looking for progress toward those outcomes. Note improved performances as well as what you believe may be ways of improving performance. You may want to use a form to remind you of factors you want to observe. **Form 9-8** provides an example of an anecdotal form, but by all means make a form you might find more useful.

Checklist of Critical Behaviors

You can use a checklist to facilitate your observations. A checklist is most commonly used to assess skills in performing procedures. Procedure manuals in your agency should describe step-by-step procedures that you can use to check off the critical behaviors required for a safe performance of procedures. You may also want to use a checklist to keep track of procedure skills your preceptee has performed or needs to perform. You may want to use identified desired outcomes as a kind of checklist, checking off outcomes and commenting on progress.

Preceptee Journaling

Reflection is a very effective learning tool. It can stimulate analysis of events enhancing memories that can guide future action in similar situations. It should also facilitate developing a habit of self-direction. Depending on your preceptee's experience and skill, you may want to vary how much you structure the journaling. You could be very directive, asking the preceptee to reflect about specific factors such as observations about the patient, decisions that were made, strengths and weaknesses of actions taken, and so forth. You might not want to be as prescriptive; just ask the preceptee to comment on events during a shift that involved decision making, or even give no specific directions other than asking for analysis of events and decision making. In these journals you can then see indicators of developing behaviors and use them for discussions with the preceptee. **Form 1-3** in Chapter 1 shows a sample journal format.

Conferences

Conferencing is a form of reflection. It serves the same purpose as written reflection. Conferences are a crucial process in precepting and in assessment. It provides opportunities to discover how your preceptee is thinking and processing learning experiences and to give feedback about progress and for your preceptee to discuss self-assessment of skill progression. It also serves as an opportunity to plan with your preceptee for ways of strengthening performance. You may want to have a short conference at the beginning of the shift to plan early activities. You may also want to meet at the end of the shift to discuss what has happened, to give feedback about strengths, and to plan for improvements.

Demonstration

Observing a preceptee perform nursing activities that demonstrate skills is another way to assess progression. Examples of this could be observing the preceptee perform a technical procedure, seeing a sample of documentation, or seeing a written nursing care plan. It is also important to ask the preceptee to self-evaluate these products or behaviors and for you to give your assessment feedback.

Questioning

Questioning about what the preceptee is thinking, planning, or doing gives you a view of skill progression. For example, right after report at the beginning of a shift, you might ask what concerns the preceptee has about assigned patients. You might also ask what questions the preceptee has about these concerns or about how these questions could be answered (if you believe the preceptee has the requisite knowledge to answer). You may ask the preceptee to decide about one or two priorities after an initial assessment of assigned patients. Avoid a challenging approach when you question. Use questioning in situations when you believe the preceptee has the ability to reflect, to analyze, and to think critically to arrive at an answer. This should help to build confidence and provide evidence of effective progression.

Role Play

Role play can be used to assess abilities. It can be used as a way to evaluate how the preceptee might act in particular situations. It may also help the preceptee anticipate potential responses to commonly occurring events on your unit. Beginners often have difficulty anticipating future possibilities. You or the preceptee can set up situations and then have the preceptee describe potential responses to the situations. You could use the same event with differing possible turns of events. You can also offer the opportunity to repeat the scenario but have the preceptee improve on the previous response. Of course, you should facilitate self-evaluation and give feedback about your observations.

Preceptor Strategies

Working With the Beginning Nurse

1. Establish clear behavioral goals and objectives.
2. Assess for expected performances (observe) described in the goals and objectives.
3. Work continually to gradually improve behavior.
    a. Use assessment tools as appropriate—anecdotal notes, checklists, conferences, demonstration, questioning, and role play.
    b. Collaborate with the preceptee to plan for strengthening and improving performance.
    c. Be honest and open about your evaluations of the preceptee. Do not inflate your evaluations or ignore preceptee weaknesses.
    d. Include all stakeholders in planning for expected performance and in assessing preceptee performance.
    e. Use continuous interaction between you and the preceptee.
    f. Use facilitative approaches with your preceptee to plan and implement progression:
        i.   Coaching
        ii. Encouraging
        iii. Supporting
        iv. Acting as a resource guide
        v.   Being available to the preceptee
        vi. Ensuring preceptee is ready to perform assignments
        vii. Encouraging reflection and self-evaluation

viii.   Using constructive communication

ix.   Avoiding over or under supervising

x.   Increasing complexity or difficulty in situations, gradually moving from simple to complex

xi.   Build trust so preceptee feels safe to engage in critical reflection

g.   Consider your preceptee's learning styles and adult learning preferences.

Working With the Experienced Nurse

There are few alterations to be made in assessment when your preceptee is more experienced than the new nurse or student. You would use the same assessment processes and tools. You would work together with the preceptee to develop goals and objectives. Probably the main difference in your approach is to be sure to identify skills the preceptee already has so you can start achieving goals at an appropriate level. You should see more self-direction and more rapid improvement in skills than with a new employee or student. You will probably need to assist less with procedures except for those unique to your unit.

Summary

It is important to be sure about what you want the preceptee to know and be able to do so you can work to develop and improve those factors. In this chapter we focused on four assessment processes. To assist you in these approaches, several assessment tools and strategies have been described. As you use them, you should enjoy seeing the progress your preceptee is making.

Reflection

- Refer to the section in the beginning of this chapter called Questions to Guide Your Learning. After completing this chapter, see if you can answer the questions. Some suggested answers are included in Appendix A.

- How do you feel when you know you are going to be assessed or evaluated by a supervisor? What could be done during assessment that would help you feel positive about the experience?

- When you think about your precepting roles, are you satisfied with your approaches? What areas of behavior do you want to work on to improve? What help do you need or want to accomplish this improvement?

- Think about your preceptee's skill progression. Identify improvements that have been achieved. What plans do you have for helping with continued improvement? Is your preceptee able to identify improvements in skills? If not, it would be helpful to point out improvements you have observed. How can you encourage the preceptee to develop plans for further improvement?

- Are you and the preceptee working well together? Have you identified his or her learning preferences? Do they match yours? If not, how have you adjusted your approach to the preceptee?

- What preceptee behavior is troubling you? Have you shared your concerns with the preceptee? How can you get the preceptee involved in planning for changes?

- Have you tried some form of written expectation planning? How has that helped to influence or modify behaviors?

- In what ways have you acted to encourage your preceptee to be self-directing?

- How have you worked with various stakeholders in your environment? Have they been collaborative and helpful? If not, what might you do? How is the preceptee working with others on the unit team? Do you need to do anything to improve that collaboration?

- When you see a need to correct a preceptee's behavior, how do you communicate this to your preceptee or help the preceptee to discover it?

References

Bastable, S. (2003). *Nurse as educator: Principles of teaching and learning for nursing practice* (2nd ed.). Sudbury, MA: Jones and Bartlett.

Gaberson, K. B., & Oermann, M. H. (2007). *Clinical teaching strategies in nursing* (2nd ed.). New York: Springer.

Gronlund, N. E. (2006). *Assessment of student achievement* (8th ed.). Boston: Allyn & Bacon.

Mager, R. (1997). *Preparing instructional objectives: A critical tool in the development of effective instruction* (3rd ed.). Atlanta, GA: Center for Effective Performance.

Palomba, C. A., & Banta, T. W. (1999). *Assessment essentials: Planning, implementing, and improving assessment in higher education.* San Francisco: Jossey-Bass.

Romiszowski, A. (1999). The development of physical skills: Instruction in the psychomotor domain. In C. M. Reigeluth (Ed.), *Instructional design theories and models: A new paradigm of instructional theory* (Vol. 2, pp. 457–481). Mahwah, NJ: Lawrence Erlbaum.

Simpson, E. (1972). *The classification of educational objectives in the psychomotor domain: The psychomotor domain* (Vol. 3). Washington, DC: Gryphon House.

Zvacek, S. M. (1999). What's my grade? Assessing learner progress. *Technology Trends, 43,* 38–43.

NOTES

FORM 9-1: PRECEPTOR EVALUATION OF PRECEPTEE

Preceptee Name _____

Preceptor Name _____ Unit in Agency _____

Date of Review _____

Please complete the following assessment of your preceptee.

Code: (1) Poor, (2) Fair, (3) Good, (4) Excellent. Place a check mark in appropriate column.

Area of Practice	1	2	3	4	Examples
Safety of nursing practice (Note you can substitute other areas of practice)					
Organizational ability					
Patient teaching ability					
Ability to work with others					
Skills in therapeutic nursing interventions (basic and commonly occurring on your unit)					
Interpersonal communication					
Judgment/decision making					

FORM 9-1: PRECEPTOR EVALUATION OF PRECEPTEE (CONTINUED)

Area of Practice	1	2	3	4	Examples
Initiative					
Written care plans					
Progression in self-direction					
Acceptance of supervision					
Patient–family interaction					
Participation as health team member					
Openness to others' beliefs					
Demonstration of professional behavior					
Appropriate use of organizational system					
Use of feedback					
Delegation ability					

(continues)

FORM 9-1: PRECEPTOR EVALUATION OF PRECEPTEE (CONTINUED)

Area of Practice	1	2	3	4	Examples
Time management					
Additional Remarks					
Areas to Focus Growth					
Areas of Strength					
Plans for Improvement					

FORM 9-2: PRECEPTEE SELF-EVALUATION

Preceptee Name _____

Preceptor Name _____ Unit in Agency _____

Date of Review _____

Please complete the following assessment of your preceptee.

Code: (1) Poor, (2) Fair, (3) Good, (4) Excellent. Place a check mark in appropriate column.

Area of Practice	1	2	3	4	Examples of Strength and Needed Growth
Safety of nursing practice (Note you can substitute other areas of practice)					
Organizational ability					
Patient teaching ability					
Ability to work with others					
Skills in therapeutic nursing interventions (basic and commonly occurring on your unit)					
Interpersonal communication					
Judgment/decision making					

(continues)

FORM 9-2: PRECEPTEE SELF-EVALUATION (CONTINUED)

Area of Practice	1	2	3	4	Examples of Strength and Needed Growth
Initiative					
Written care plans					
Progression in self-direction					
Acceptance of supervision					
Patient–family interaction					
Participation as health team member					
Openness to others' beliefs					
Demonstration of professional behavior					
Appropriate use of organizational system					
Use of feedback					

FORM 9-2: PRECEPTEE SELF-EVALUATION (CONTINUED)

Area of Practice	1	2	3	4	Examples of Strength and Needed Growth
Delegation ability					
Time management					

Additional Remarks

_____

_____

_____

_____

_____

_____

Areas to Focus Growth

_____

_____

_____

_____

_____

_____

(continues)

FORM 9-2: PRECEPTEE SELF-EVALUATION (CONTINUED)

Areas of Strength

_____

_____

_____

_____

Plans for Improvement

_____

_____

_____

_____

FORM 9-3: PRECEPTEE EVALUATION OF PRECEPTOR

Preceptor Name _____   Preceptee _____

Clinical Unit _____   Date _____

Code: (1) Poor, (2) Fair, (3) Good, (4) Excellent. Place a check mark in the appropriate column.

Area of Evaluation	1	2	3	4	Examples
My preceptor serves as an expert professional role model.					
My preceptor involved me in developing goals and objectives for this experience.					
My preceptor and I developed daily and weekly objectives and plans.					
My preceptor assists in planning and arranging assignments and activities to meet learning objectives.					
My preceptor provides feedback about progress in an ongoing manner.					
My preceptor encourages me to be self-directed.					
My preceptor appropriately assesses my skill capabilities and allows me to perform skills.					

(continues)

FORM 9-3: PRECEPTEE EVALUATION OF PRECEPTOR (CONTINUED)

Area of Evaluation	1	2	3	4	Examples
My preceptor supervises me directly when needed.					
My preceptor evaluates me in a positive, constructive manner.					
My preceptor's clinical knowledge was accurate.					
My preceptor actively sought educational opportunities to meet my learning needs.					
My preceptor was available when I needed help.					
My preceptor helped me fit in with the work group on the unit.					
My preceptor presented information in a logical clear manner.					
I was comfortable asking questions.					
My preceptor communicated with me by actively listening and asking me for input.					
My preceptor was consistently pleasant and helpful.					

FORM 9-3: PRECEPTEE EVALUATION OF PRECEPTOR (CONTINUED)

Area of Evaluation	1	2	3	4	Examples
The amount of supervision I received from my preceptor was always appropriate.					

What I found most helpful was

_____

_____

_____

_____

_____

_____

I would like it if my preceptor did the following:

_____

_____

_____

_____

_____

_____

FORM 9-4: CHECKLIST FOR EFFECTIVE OBJECTIVES

Check Observable Behavior

Is an observable behavior described?

Is the behavior the key or most important desired behavior?

Is the key desired behavior clear?

If the behavior is not observable, is an observable behavior stated?

Check Behavior Specifications, Limitations, Provisions, or Requirements

If applicable:

Is there a description of what the learner will be given, or be deprived of, during performance?

Have all specifications, limitations, provisions, or requirements that influence demonstrated behavior been described?

Expected Standards

Is there a description of how well the learner must perform?

Is the described expected standard realistic; can it be achieved in the expected time frame?

FORM 9-5: EXPECTATION PLANNING

Expectations Goals and Objectives	Plans for Developing Skills	Target Date	Progress

FORM 9-6: IMPROVEMENT PLANNING

Behavior Targeted for Improvement	Plans for Developing Improved Skills	Target Date	Progress

FORM 9-7: DAILY PLANNING SHEET

Today's Objectives Include behaviors needing improvement from previous experiences or new experiences you want to seek out.	Specific Plans for Achieving Objectives	Assessment of Objective Achievements Note needed improvements or needed experiences for next day.

FORM 9-8: ANECDOTAL NOTE FORM

Date	Objective Daily or Final	Observations Describe Situation and Behaviors	Action Plan

CHAPTER TEN

Launching Your Precepting Experience and Tracking Progress

> The world is round and the place which may seem like the end may also be the beginning.
>
> —**Ivy Baker Priest**

INTRODUCTION

Assuming that you've completed a preceptor development course or that you've completed this workbook on your own, you're ready to receive your preceptee. We hope you feel ready to start this important journey in which you will be a supportive resource, guide, coach, and teacher and be vitally important in helping your preceptee transition as a beginning nurse or an experienced nurse to someone you want to work with on your unit. One purpose of this chapter is to offer a brief review of key preceptor strategies discussed in each chapter. We are sure you will feel proud of what you have accomplished when you finish a precepting experience. Another purpose for this chapter is to describe some potential ways of dealing with some selected problems you could encounter. Finally, we want to help you take a reflective look back to assess your precepting experiences. We offer a format for doing that assessment.

OBJECTIVES

After completing the chapter and related learning activities, you should be able to

1. Describe key strategies for each chapter in the book.
2. Develop and use appropriate preceptor strategies while working with an assigned preceptee.
3. Describe one appropriate way of responding to identified preceptor problems.
4. Assess (complete **Form 10-1**) your precepting process after completing one precepting cycle.

QUESTIONS TO GUIDE YOUR LEARNING

1. What are five roles you will perform as you precept?

2. What are four legal considerations you should attend to as a preceptor?

3. What is your liability when working with a preceptee?

4. What will most affect your decision to assign patients to your preceptee?

5. What key personnel will you want to introduce to your preceptee early in the precepting experience?

6. Your preceptee has just graduated from a basic nursing program. He exhibits common beginner behaviors. Choose three beginner behaviors, and describe how you will work with each.

7. Organization is a problem when someone is new to a situation. What is one strategy you might use to help your preceptee organize at the beginning of a shift?

8. What is a preceptor strategy that applies to the following principle of adult learning: readiness to learn is influenced by the need to know or be able to do something?

9. Your preceptee is an assimilator, whereas you are an accommodator. What is one potential problem in working with this preceptee?

10. The preceptee may be motivated to learn but may have some anxiety about the clinical experience. How will you help the preceptee gain confidence and maintain motivation?

11. What are six components that create a safe learning environment within the complex environment of health care?

12. Your preceptee is culturally different from you. What three things can you do to enhance your cultural awareness?

13. The preceptor is a "Baby Boomer" and the preceptee is a "Nexter." Even though the work day is complete you notice the preceptor remains on the unit to chat with a physician as the preceptee leaves to attend Pilates class. What are two examples of generational diversity shown in this scenario?

14. What are four strategies you can use to assess your preceptee's performance?

15. Your student preceptee is quiet. She asks almost no questions, and she makes many mistakes in performing procedures even though you have repeatedly helped her with the procedures. What are three actions you should take if you believe she should not pass the precepted experience?

Key Strategies Discussed in Each Chapter

For each chapter in the book, a brief description is provided of preceptor strategies for dealing with a student nurse, a beginning nurse, or an experienced nurse. More details are described within the chapters; however, this should help you remember key strategies.

Chapter One: Roles and Responsibilities

1. Know who is involved in the precepting experience. Make certain that they know their roles and responsibilities and how they relate to new employees or to students. Verify your own roles as well.

2. Meet together to clarify roles and responsibilities.

3. Share contact information including e-mail addresses, telephone numbers, cell phone numbers, and off-hour contact information.

4. If your preceptee is a student, make certain that you have contact information for both the substitute faculty supervisor and the school of nursing administrator should the supervising faculty member be unavailable.

5. Validate understandings throughout the experience.

6. Initial and ongoing communication must be clear, specific, objective, and constructive.

7. Be enthusiastic as you work with the preceptee.

8. Be positive and supportive.

Chapter Two: Legal and Regulatory Considerations

1. Ensure appropriate orientation.

2. Use chapter checklist, Form 2-1, to guide you through legal and regulatory requirements.

3. Dispel the common misconception that the preceptee is "working under your license." You, the preceptee, and other personnel are held accountable for behaviors expected of a person with a license or those of a student at a particular level in an education program.

4. Be sure to supervise your preceptee. Your liability rests with appropriate supervision and appropriate assignment.

5. Delegate only after you have apprised yourself of your preceptee's ability to perform the task.

6. Know those tasks or procedures that require advance certification. They may be different for schools of nursing.

7. Ensure any needed contracts are negotiated before you start.

Chapter Three: Getting Started

1. Know your organization and how you successfully operate within the organization.

2. Identify key personnel that have an influence on your ability to get work done.

3. Plan carefully for setting the stage when you first meet the preceptee. The first meeting is one of the most crucial. It launches the experience.

4. Plan for a detailed orientation to the unit and people working on the unit.

5. Meet in an environment that allows for casual, uninterrupted initial dialogue.

6. Maintain enthusiasm for working with the preceptee.

7. Encourage ongoing dialogue throughout the day. Establish an environment in which it is safe to critique events.

8. Introduce your preceptee to key personnel.

9. Wrap up each day with 5 minutes of uninterrupted time with your preceptee reflecting about the day's events.

10. Provide your preceptee with timely feedback. Celebrate and reward successes.

11. Use the forms included in the chapter to assist you in helping your preceptee get off to a good start.

Chapter Four: Working With Beginners

1. Remember that experiences and reflection about experiences is what generates skill progression.

2. Assess your preceptee's skill level.

   a. If your preceptee is a beginner, know the typical characteristics of beginner behavior. Review beginner behaviors and hints for working with beginners in Chapter 4.

   b. If you are working with experienced nurses, they can be beginners in your environment and exhibit some of the same beginner behaviors. The experienced nurse should progress more rapidly than a beginner.

3. Assess your skill level from competent to expert.

4. Bridge the gap between your and your preceptee's skill levels.

   a. Be patient and supportive. Offer assistance as necessary.

   b. Offer clear, complete, specific, constructive feedback about experiences.

   c. Encourage questions, and support your preceptee's reflective exploration of answers.

   d. Make time in the day for reflection and dialogue about experiences.

   e. Verify your preceptee's skill progression.

5. Maintain stability in the work environment.

   a. Ensure that your preceptee works with you rather than a number of others.

   b. Work consecutive days when possible so that the preceptee can build on previous experiences.

6. Reflection enhances learning and progression Keep your preceptee actively engaged in reflecting about their experiences.

Chapter Five: Helping With Time Management

1. Offer guidance in organizing activities.
2. Encourage the development of and use of work planning sheets.
3. Start the shift with a plan and help to reorganize as the need arises throughout the shift.
4. Help in setting realistic time lines.
5. Help with anticipating patient responses to illness and treatments.
6. Help your preceptee identify both internal and external time wasters and ways of minimizing them.

Chapter Six: Adult Learning and Learning Styles

1. Use strategies appropriate for adult learning.
   a. Allow for and encourage self-direction.
   b. Always treat your preceptee with respect. Promote your preceptee's feelings of adequacy, competency, and security.
   c. Use your preceptee's previous learning to enhance or connect it to learning in new situations.
   d. Consider your preceptee's need to learn, which strongly affects readiness to learn.
   e. Explain or help your preceptee understand reasons for learning something; make it clear why knowing or being able to do something is valuable.
   f. Establish relevance of the skill taught by providing rationale and linking it to a role or work.
2. Use strategies for learning style variations.
   a. People have preferred ways of taking in and processing information. Help your preceptee to self-assess his or her learning styles. Assess your preferred ways of taking in and processing information.
   b. Use a variety of strategies when presenting new information.
   c. Use each other's learning style strengths when working together.

Chapter Seven: Keeping Your Preceptee Motivated

1. Motivation varies per individual.
   a. Reflect on the values and beliefs that maintain you in your nursing role.

    b. Discuss your preceptee's values and beliefs about nursing.

    c. Maintain open dialogue with your preceptee while validating his or her feelings about the nursing profession.

    d. Help your preceptee set realistic goals.

    e. Help your preceptee break big tasks into small ones.

    f. Encourage reflection and validate self-assessments.

2. Context affects motivation.

    a. Maintain motivation by making certain the environment is "safe" for learning.

    b. Model competency.

    c. Communicate openly.

    d. Point out the positive.

Chapter Eight: Working With Diversity

1. To demonstrate cultural congruence is to recognize cultural differences, sensitivities, and priorities.

2. Cultural differences are not limited to race and ethnicity but may also include age, gender, religion, sexual orientation, mental or physical abilities, and educational level.

3. Cultural framework is shaped by life experiences. Learn about the preceptee through dialogue and shared communication.

4. Identify relevant artifacts and compare the stated with that which is observed when assessing your organization's cultural congruence.

5. Integrate cultural awareness, cultural knowledge skill development, and learn from each cultural encounter when developing culturally congruent skills.

6. Be aware of generational differences in values and beliefs about work, collaboration, and lifestyle.

7. Be aware of differences in cultural context between internationally educated nurses and nurses educated in the United States.

Chapter Nine: Assessment

1. Continuously use all four assessment processes.

    a. Collaborate with your preceptee to establish clear goals and objectives for the precepting period, for a month, week, and each day.

    b. Collaborate with your preceptee to develop strategies that facilitate goal and objective achievement.

    c. Observe for desired behaviors or outcomes, using several possible strategies such as anecdotal notes, discussions, questioning, role playing, written logs, and skill performances.

    d. Make judgments about the quality of behaviors you observed and plan for improving and strengthening what you saw.

2. Use constructive facilitative approaches when interacting with your preceptee.

Dealing with Problems You May Encounter

Anticipating and preventing problems with the precepting process is important for a smooth experience with your preceptee. This section briefly describes approaches to situations in which your preceptee is failing; you are experiencing negative behaviors from your manager, peers, or other staff; when you and your preceptee are not a good match; and when you've been assigned to precept and don't really want to do it again right now.

Strategies When You Experience Uncooperative or Obstructive Behaviors in Your Peers or Other Staff Members

1. Again, prevention is the best strategy. All parties involved in the precepting experience should collaborate to reach agreement on policies and procedures. When the manager or agency makes decisions about these matters, without collaboration, this frequently leads to serious problems.

2. Other staff members may resent that you are devoting so much time to the preceptee and may become obstructive, such as expecting you to take an extra heavy assignment because you have "help" or acting inappropriately with the preceptee. Discuss what you are doing with them, clearly articulate your needs, and reiterate that you will more likely need extra time to work with your preceptee instead of extra work. Discuss with your manager your need for a reduced workload to be an effective preceptor.

3. Involve nurse managers and agency educators in assisting with conflict resolution and providing educational resources.

Strategies for Appropriate Preceptor Selection

1. First, a preceptor should be willing to do the job and have the abilities to facilitate student or new employee learning experiences. You should not just be appointed as a preceptor. Collaborate with your colleagues to reach agreement on an equitable selection process. You might consider a self-selection approach that attempts to more closely match your skills and personality with your preceptee's. Avoid preceptor selection based primarily on availability.

2. Negotiate selection based on skill, experience and education, and a thorough preceptor orientation. All preceptors should complete preceptor classes/orientation.

3. If you have precepted several times in a row and would like a break from the role, let your manager know this. This need for a break is very common, particularly when there are too few prepared preceptors. Perhaps you could involve a few preceptors in an ongoing support group. Sharing suggestions with this group could be very helpful.

4. You may feel insecure about your ability to be an effective preceptor, collaborate with other preceptors in your agency. Ask for assistance and ideas.

Strategies When Your Preceptee Is Performing Poorly or Failing

Obviously, it would be best to prevent behaviors that are unacceptable; however, there are times when, in spite of trying to avoid failure, the preceptee's skill progression and behavior is unacceptable. When you see the failure unfolding, it can be very stressful (Hrobsky & Kersbergen, 2002). You may feel like a failure or you may be fearful of patient harm. You may be reluctant to report unacceptable behavior for many reasons, but you do need to take action. What can you do? Minimize the problem by making expectations clear and continuously evaluating performance and offering timely constructive feedback so there are opportunities for the preceptee to remediate.

1. Ensure that you are clear about expected outcomes for your preceptee. Verify them with your agency or the school of nursing.

2. When you see inappropriate behaviors, such as unsuitable communications with patients, poor grooming, and arriving for the shift late, discuss the behaviors with the preceptee in a private environment. Encourage the preceptee to explain the behavior. There could be problems with events outside the clinical situation that prevent acceptable behaviors. Work with the preceptee to solve these problems if possible. Plan for specific improved behaviors.

3. When you see failure warning flags, such as the preceptee asks little or no questions, has a lack of enthusiasm for nursing, a dull affect, or repeatedly demonstrating unsatisfactory clinical skills, take action as soon as you are aware of the warnings. Don't wait, hoping for improvement.

    a. If the preceptee is a student, convene a meeting with the student and the faculty liaison immediately.

    b. If your preceptee is a new employee, discuss the behaviors with the preceptee and your manager as soon as possible.

    c. Ask the preceptee to complete a self-evaluation using the learning goals and objectives as benchmarks for evaluation.

    d. Make a remediation plan with the preceptee and faculty liaison (student) or manager (new employee).

    e. Be an advocate for quality patient care. Condoning failing behavior is inconsistent with your role as patient advocate. You may experience feelings of responsibility for preceptee failure. Do not concede your role; protect patients first.

    f. Keep anecdotal notes and be able to describe examples of unacceptable behaviors using specific examples. Be as objective as possible. Be sure you are neither too lenient nor too severe in your evaluations. If unsure of the language you're using in the evaluation, collaborate with your manager, the faculty liaison, or another preceptor for support.

4. If you have a marginal or failing student you will probably find that you spend increasing time ensuring safe practices. Share your concerns with your manager.

Assessing Your Precepting Experiences

While you are precepting and after you have been through one precepting experience, it is important to reflect about what was fulfilling for you, or pleasing, or successful as well as those events that were negative or unsuccessful. This is particularly important for your first time because it can offer insights for subsequent precepting experiences. Assessing your experiences will be more effective if you have written reflective impressions frequently during the precepting time. If you don't do this your impressions may fade or become diluted, or you may forget them. Include in your assessment

- The quality of your preparation for the preceptor roles
- Skills you developed in your roles
- Skills that were problematic
- Stresses during the process: your own, problems presented by the preceptee, workload, peer acceptance, or organization
- Activities and strategies that worked well
- Activities and strategies that were problematic
- Reflection on what you would do differently next time you precept

You can use **Form 10-1** as a guide to assessing your experiences.

Summary

This chapter offers a review of important preceptor strategies for each chapter in the book and discusses some potential problems you may encounter in your role as well as some suggestions that may assist you in managing them. This chapter also offers an assessment guide for you to use as you reflect about your precepting experiences. Based on the information, you may make adjustments for the next precepting cycle. We wish you many enriching experiences in your journey.

Reflection

- Refer to the section in the beginning of this chapter called Questions to Guide Your Learning. After completing this chapter, see if you can answer the questions. Some suggested answers are included in Appendix A.
- What has been done to orient the staff on your unit about your preceptor roles? What can you do to reinforce their understanding?
- Appropriate preceptee assignments and supervision are critical for protecting your liability. How can you determine an appropriate assignment?
- What do you want to include in your first preceptee meeting?
- Your preceptee needs an orientation. Outline a plan that includes topics you want to cover and objectives you want to achieve. Develop a timeline for strategies that incorporate those topics.
- What diagnoses are common on your unit? What critical information do you want your preceptee to know about these diagnoses? How will you proceed to teach these factors?
- What is your level of skill progression? How can you bridge the gap between your skill and your preceptee's?
- Pick four beginner behaviors and describe one way you plan to work with that behavior.
- Describe two ways you plan to help your preceptee deal with external time wasters.
- When you are learning something new, what motivates you to work at that? What are two ways you can apply adult learning principles?
- How will you assess your preceptee's favored learning style? If your styles tend to be in opposition, what is one strategy you can use to enhance learning?
- Your preceptee believes she should be able to perform as a competent nurse, but she is a new nurse without practical experience. She sees that she is not confident about her skills and is questioning her ability to become competent. What are two things you could do to improve her motivation to continue in her endeavor and to improve?
- What diversities do you see in your preceptee? How do you plan to deal with them?
- How will you start your assessment in each of the four assessment processes?
- What are four assessment strategies you might use to make a decision about your preceptee's progression?
- You have been precepting for 2 weeks. You notice that some of the staff members are resentful of the extra time you are taking with your preceptee, expecting them to take up the slack. What is one way you could prevent this from happening and what is one way to start dealing with the problem?
- How were you selected to become a preceptor? What would you do if you were appointed to the role and you didn't want to be a preceptor for a while?
- What are some warning signs of pending preceptee failure? What is one way of preventing failure and how would you proceed when you observe inappropriate behaviors?

Reference

Hrobsky, P. E., & Kersbergen, A. L. (2002). Preceptors' perceptions of clinical performance failure. *Journal of Nursing Education, 41,* 550–553.

NOTES

FORM 10-1: ASSESSING YOUR PRECEPTING EXPERIENCE

As you progress through the precepting experience, reflect about the following aspects. Provide some specific examples (things that are standouts about your experiences), and write plans you have for strengthening or improving these in the future.

Using this rating scale, write the number that best rates your satisfaction in the items below

Highly Unsatisfactory 1   2   3   4   5   Highly Satisfactory

Precepting Experiences	Rating	Examples and Plans
Your preparation for the preceptor roles		
Your responsibilities related to legal and regulatory considerations		
Orienting your preceptee to the experience		
Working with beginner behaviors		
Your responsibilities related to legal and regulatory considerations		

(continues)

FORM 10-1: ASSESSING YOUR PRECEPTING EXPERIENCE (CONTINUED)

Precepting Experiences	Rating	Examples and Plans
Facilitating your preceptee's time management skill development		
Applying adult learning principles with your preceptee		
Using strategies that facilitate your preceptee's learning styles		
Using preceptor strategies that are motivating for your preceptee		
Using preceptor strategies that develop cultural congruence in you and your preceptee		
Assessing your preceptee's skill progression		

FORM 10-1: ASSESSING YOUR PRECEPTING EXPERIENCE (CONTINUED)

What are examples of experiences that were particularly successful or satisfying for you as you progressed through the precepting process?

Successful	Plans for Strengthening

(continues)

FORM 10-1: ASSESSING YOUR PRECEPTING EXPERIENCE (CONTINUED)

What are examples of experiences that were particularly stressful or unsatisfactory for you?

Successful	Plans for Improving or Changing

APPENDIX A

Answers to Chapter Questions

Answers to Questions for Chapter One:
What Everyone Should Be Doing: Roles and Responsibilities

Questions to Guide Your Learning

1. Are you able to identify the participants who are facilitating your preceptee's experiences?

   If your preceptee is a student, you will be meeting with the student and the supervising faculty member. However, there are other people within the school of nursing and your hospital that have an indirect responsibility for the success of the preceptor program. Know the chain of command at the school of nursing that includes the course coordinator and the dean or director of the school.

   If your preceptee is a new employee or a student, it is important to know the agency participants. These people may include members of the staff development department or the education department, staff from human resources, and from administration.

2. Do you know the roles and responsibilities of each of the participants?

   Communicate with each of the major participants to facilitate the preceptee experiences. Clarify any misconceptions or miscommunication in a timely manner.

3. What are the roles and responsibilities of the preceptor?

   The role of preceptor is multifaceted and integrates the roles of coach, teacher, facilitator, resource person, and evaluator. These roles are consistent when working with both students and new employees.

   As a coach, you will be directing and guiding your preceptee's learning experiences. As a teacher you will manage the learning possibilities provided through many different learning experiences sought out by you. As a facilitator you will guide and supervise your preceptee's journey through the routines, protocols, and culture of your unit and organization. Help your preceptee gain the knowledge of both the formal and informal network of how things get done. Helping your preceptee discover the people, equipment, and materials needed to complete projects or a task is integral to your role as a resource. Finally, you will be responsible for evaluating both your preceptee's progress and the success of the preceptor program.

4. How will you help your preceptee maximize learning experiences when planning for daily activities?

   Collaboratively determine the day's learning priorities. Assess and validate your preceptee's plan for goal achievement using the Preceptor Planning Guide. Provide timely feedback throughout the day. Help your preceptee manage problems or challenges that arise during the day's activities. Encourage your preceptee to evaluate progress and provide validating feedback. Meet with your preceptee at the end of the shift to summarize highlights and to set goals for the upcoming experience.

5. Why meet with your preceptee at the end of the shift/work day? What will you talk about?

   Set aside 15 minutes at the end of the shift or work day to summarize the activities and events of the day. Discuss the things that went well and the activities and behaviors that presented a challenge. Discuss future strategies that may strengthen the behaviors that led to positive outcomes. Analyze the behaviors that were challenging and help your preceptee explore different ways of doing or behaving that will result in positive outcomes.

6. How will you respond if you believe you are not a "good match" for your preceptee?

   Generally, preceptor–preceptee relationships thrive as trust, respect, and communication patterns develop. In the rare instance where a mismatch occurs, contact the faculty supervisor, if the preceptee is a student. Meet with the student and the faculty supervisor to discuss, with objectivity, the situation. If the preceptee is a new employee, meet with the unit manager, the preceptee, and the director of the preceptor program. Share objective data that support your request to abort the relationship.

7. What is the purpose of your preceptee's reflective journal?

   The reflective journal is a tool designed to stimulate critical and creative thinking. Thinking about experiences gives access to and constructs meaning from experience. It enhances memory for applying past experiences to new similar experiences.

8. Why is reflective journaling an effective strategy for maximizing learning?

   Reflective journaling is a learning strategy that allows for critical thinking and evaluation. The journal is a source of information from which the preceptee can create hypotheses, rehearse interactions or interventions, and evaluate behavioral outcomes. It is a synthesis of thought and feelings about experienced scenarios.

9. Is it appropriate to share your preceptee's reflective journal with your colleagues?

   The reflective journal is typically the property of the preceptee and is usually kept confidential. It is the preceptee's decision to share it with you. It is your responsibility to garner the permission of the preceptee before sharing any entries with colleagues.

10. Who is responsible for evaluating the employee preceptee?

    This is predetermined at the onset of the preceptorship. Expect to contribute information to the comprehensive evaluation set forth in the preceptorship policies and procedures. Be cognizant of required assessments and time frames for reporting. Review this with the director of the preceptor program and the preceptee during your initial meeting.

Answers to Questions for Chapter Two: Considering Legal and Regulatory Controls

Questions to Guide Your Learning

1. Do you understand both your and your preceptee's roles and responsibilities?

    These should be spelled out in your agency's policies for new graduate or employee orientation. If you are working with a student, the roles should be clearly described in the contract between you, the preceptee, and the clinical faculty supervisor. If they are not, ask for clarification.

2. Do you meet your state, agency, or school of nursing preceptor qualifications?

    This should appear in your state's Nurse Practice Act. A school of nursing may have additional qualifications.

3. Must the preceptee always work directly under your supervision? Can you assign the preceptee to another registered nurse or staff member?

    Check with your agency policies and/or the school of nursing policies. If you are not able to work with the preceptee for 1 or 2 days, it is probably best to ask the preceptee to wait until you are back working in the agency. If you need to be away for several days, it is probably best to ask for another nurse to take over your precepting roles. If your preceptee is a student, that substitute should add her signature to the contract between her or him and the school of nursing.

4. What orientation has been provided for the preceptee? What additional information is needed for orientation to the agency and to the particular unit in the agency?

    Find out what kind of orientation your agency offers, and when it is offered. You may want to make arrangements for either attending an on-site orientation or completing other agency orientations such as watching a video or DVD and possibly a test or demonstration of skills.

5. Has the preceptee received HIPAA and OSHA orientation? If not, what arrangements for appropriate orientation are needed? How can you make it happen before you start with your preceptee?

    Same answer as for question 4.

6. Have you checked the status of your preceptee's license? Is the preceptee fully licensed, an interim permitee, or an unlicensed nursing student?

    The most important factor here is that the preceptee holds a current valid license. If the preceptee is a student, be sure the student is registered for the semester or quarter with a school of nursing.

7. What is your liability as a preceptor during precepted experiences? What is your preceptee's liability?

    Each of you is held accountable for behaviors expected of a person with a license or those of a student. You are liable for adequate supervision and for appropriately assigning responsibilities and activities. You need to observe your preceptee to be sure he or she is performing at a safe effective level. You need to be sure the preceptee is able to safely perform the activities and procedures assigned or delegated.

8. Are there any technical procedures the preceptee is not permitted to perform because certification is necessary or because the preceptee is a student and the school or agency doesn't allow students to perform these procedures?

    Check your agency policies. If there are required certifications, make arrangements for these and/or verify they are completed. Work with the clinical faculty supervisor to identify any procedures for which students need certification or may not perform.

9. May a student perform procedures requiring agency certification under your direct supervision? For those procedures requiring demonstrated competence, which can your preceptee perform?

    Check your agency policies and your preceptee's experience. If the preceptee is a student, also ask the faculty supervisor what the school of nursing requires.

10. Is there any documentation completed by the preceptee that requires your cosignature?

    Check agency policies. Check also school of nursing policies if working with a student.

11. How will you determine the amount of direct supervision needed by the preceptee?

    Discuss possibilities with the preceptee. For example, what you want to see the preceptee perform, the preceptee's past clinical experiences with procedures, and your feelings about the preceptee being free to seek your supervision or help. Check a student's clinical skills checklist. Pay particular attention to commonly occurring technical procedures.

    You probably want to supervise/observe more closely when you first begin working with the preceptee. Then, gradually, as you develop confidence in skill levels, plan with the preceptee to operate without supervision unless there are unusual circumstances.

12. If you are working with a student, have you verified the student's liability insurance and any needed health clearances? Have you signed a contract with your student if the school of nursing requires this?

    Verify requirements, both your agency requirements and the school of nursing requirements. If you are working with a student, it is helpful to have a portfolio containing verification of health clearance, liability insurance, and a copy of the contract negotiated with the school of nursing. Ask the school of nursing if they are keeping verification records.

Answers to Questions for Chapter Three: Getting Off to a Good Start

Questions to Guide Your Learning

1. What are the values of your organization? How do you see them lived in your work? What one word would describe your organization? How does the organization enable or inhibit your ability to carry out your work each day? If you encounter problems, how do you deal with them?

    Your organization's culture should reflect its values and beliefs. When thinking about this concept, reflect on what you know about the culture of your unit and of the organization as a whole. Ask yourself what values are explicit and obvious to an outsider. Then think about those things that are implicit, that may only be known by those working within the organization. Observe the artifacts. The questions posed above help to guide your thinking about the congruence between organizational values and beliefs and its culture.

2. What three things can you do to get your preceptor–preceptee relationship off to a good start? What steps will you take to optimize the chances that your preceptee is welcomed on your unit?

    Share relevant data. Plan for how you will communicate with each other. Conduct your initial meeting at a location that is void of interruptions.

    Identify people who are integral to your preceptee's ability to get work done. Introduce your preceptee to these people and share your preceptee's roles and responsibilities with them.

    Help your preceptee prepare to work on your unit by identifying and sharing commonly occurring patient diagnoses, laboratory tests, commonly prescribed medications, and routines.

    Introduce your preceptee to unit customs, such as ways of interacting with colleagues.

3. Recall your first days of working on your unit. What prominent memory of your first day of work do you have? How will you orient your preceptee to your unit? What are the four things that are most important for your preceptee to know about how your unit functions?

    Reflect on your initial days on your unit. What was good about the experience and what circumstances would you have changed. Keep these things in mind as you prepare for your preceptee's first days.

    Four pieces of information that are critical to the success of your preceptee's first few days working on the unit are knowing the people, the routines, the unit hierarchy (whom to contact for help), and things that are commonly used on your unit.

4. What knowledge, skills, procedures, and protocols will your preceptee need to know to manage the first 2 to 3 days of working with your unit team? Can you identify the team members who are integral to your preceptee's employment success?

Use the forms located at the end of Chapter 3 to guide your thinking about people, procedures, medications, and commonly occurring judgments. Share this information with your preceptee.

5. What are the most common diagnoses, medications, treatments, common judgments or decisions, and routines on your unit that you know the preceptee will definitely encounter?

Use the appropriate forms (Forms 3-2, 3-3, 3-4, 3-5, 3-6, and 3-7) at the end of the chapter to help you identify these pieces of information,

6. What strategies to you plan to facilitate your preceptee's progression? What do you need to know to help guide your preceptee's professional role development?

Collaborate on what needs to be done (learning objectives), what support is required (facilitating resource development), and how outcomes are evaluated (assessment). Assess your preceptee's skill set and level of comfort. Remember to introduce concepts, skills, or tasks that progress from simple tasks, concepts, and skills to those that are more complex. Give timely feedback.

7. What will you do if your preceptee doesn't ask questions? How will you know if your preceptee understands all the information you are sharing with him or her?

You may use focus questions to guide your preceptee's thinking. For example, the physician writes an order for potassium to be added to the patient's intravenous line. You may ask you preceptee to provide rationale for why the order was written. If your preceptee is unable to provide a hypothesis that is relevant, help your preceptee analyze the situation by asking questions such as, "What do you think you need to know to understand the reason for this order." Help the preceptee think through the patient's potassium level, how this relates to the patient's diagnosis, and what outcomes might occur after the addition of potassium to the intravenous line. Find opportunities to apply the information to a different case.

Answers to Questions for Chapter Four:
Working With Beginner Behaviors and Ways of Thinking

Questions to Guide Your Learning

1. What four factors can facilitate skill progression?
   a. Experience frequency—Arranging for frequent experiences in the same environment and for consecutive shifts.
   b. Experience stability—Arrange for working on the same shift, on the same unit.
   c. Effective feedback—Provide feedback that informs the beginner about his or her practices. Discuss events periodically during the shift and after the shift that informs the beginner about the efficacy or inefficacy of both thinking and technical skills.

d. Engagement and involvement—Encourage reflection about what went on in a situation, what one was thinking about, possibilities considered, decisions made, actions taken, and different actions that one would take if this happened again. Discuss reflective logs.

2. What are three behaviors of a beginner (new nurse, student nurse intern)?

Use the Beginner Behavior Checklist to help you identify three beginner behaviors. You might also look at the hints for working with beginners for ways to help the beginner with these behaviors.

The novice focuses totally on the immediate situation and on which skills are needed for the procedure. Many elements in the environment will be totally missed.

3. What are four ways to work with beginner behaviors to facilitate skill progression?

Refer to the hints for working with beginners and beginner strategies. For example, help your beginner with time management and organization. Encourage the beginner to discuss priorities with you and make suggestions for ways to increase efficiency. Start the shift by discussing beginner's plans. Help with anticipating future events and encourage reflection about events.

4. When a preceptee seems "frozen," that is, unable to make a decision or take action, what is one thing you could do to "unfreeze" him or her in the situation?

You could suggest the preceptee go to the break room and think about the next thing or two that needs to be done. You might suggest a next step that could be taken. Usually, after getting started the beginner's freezing stops and they are able to carry on. Another approach is to work along with the preceptee. Much depends on the situation, its complexity, and urgency. If the situation allows it and the preceptee is able, it is better to help the beginner think through what to do next rather than be told. Later in the shift, give whatever feedback you can about the situation and discuss what happened and what might be possible in a future similar situation.

5. Beginners often ask many questions. What would be a helpful response to these questions?

There are several considerations to make: the urgency of getting an answer in the situation and the type of needed information (how to do something, locating something, needed knowledge, validation of a potential decision). Assuming there is no urgency in the situation when a question is asked and involves making a decision about what to do, you might explore if the beginner is able to answer the question. If he or she can figure out what information is needed, and with your prompting, generate possibilities and select the best possibility among choices, this approach will be more helpful than supplying an answer. If the preceptee is unable to do this, try describing your thinking rather than just answering the question. Also consider preventing the need for questions by discussing areas that may be problematic or need attention early in the shift such as, "Let's see, what are some things you will need to find out about before you get started?" or "What concerns you most about your patients right now?" "What will you need to know?" "How will you get that information or who do you need to consult?" Keep in mind that questioning is a huge safety measure. Because they lack confidence, beginners usually ask before acting when they are in doubt.

Answers to Questions for Chapter Five: Helping with Time Management —

Questions to Guide Your Learning

The answers to this chapter's questions depend on circumstances on your unit. Some suggestions for answering these questions are offered.

1. What are your own time wasters?

    Identify your external and internal time wasters. Form 5-1 should help you track these wasters.

2. What are some time management strategies you use? How can you share these with your preceptee?

    Once you have identified your time wasters, describe for yourself and your preceptee what you do to minimize them. Also describe those activities you generally use to be effective in time management.

3. How do you prioritize your activities at the beginning of the shift? Have you shared this with your preceptee?

    Describe general factors such as things that must be completed within a limited time frame such as medications, things you note in report and check on soon after report, what you note on your first round of patients, and those activities you consider in anticipating events that may occur during the shift. Share these strategies with your preceptee.

4. What time management problems have you observed in your preceptee; both beginner and classic problems?

    You might use Form 5-3 to track your preceptee's problems. Be sure to discuss them with your preceptee, but remember to frame it in a way that addresses what can be done to minimize the problems rather than merely discussing what should not be happening.

5. What one strategy can you use to reduce two beginner time management problems?

    Look at the list of beginner time management problems. The tracking sheet (Form 5-3) should also be helpful. Probably one thing you need to do is check on the preceptee's planning the first thing in the shift, suggest possible changes that could be tried, observe organization and prioritization frequently during the shift, and help with reorganization as events interrupt the preceptee's routines and his or her initial plans.

6. What problems do new nurses or student nurses have with delegating?

    - Not feeling empowered to delegate.

- Feeling that needing to delegate is a sign of not being able to manage organization.

- Delegating to the wrong person (a person not permitted to perform the activity; a person with inadequate knowledge or ability to perform the activity).

- Delegating too often because of chronically falling behind and needing another's help.

- Feeling that he or she is better qualified to complete a task even though assistive personnel can legally perform the task.

7. What are two strategies you can use to refine your preceptee's classic time management problems in each of the areas below?

   a. Organizing and prioritizing

   - Orient to events peculiar to your unit that involve given time frames.

   - Help your preceptee identify potential unplanned activities that might emerge as a result of a patient's condition.

   - Work with the preceptee to develop a worksheet that helps with organizing activities.

   b. Delegating

   - When you notice that your preceptee is falling behind, work with the preceptee to identify an appropriate delegation opportunity.

   - Review legal and regulatory factors that influence appropriate delegation.

   - Discuss what the preceptee might say in communicating to a delegate.

8. What strategies for improving time management can you use when precepting a more experienced nurse?

   - Carefully orient to routines that are time-based on your unit.

   - Orient to departments with which the preceptee will need to collaborate.

   - Discuss team approaches typically used on your unit that involve time management.

   - Assess time management skills or problems. Use strategies to reduce problems as needed. Avoid being overly directive if the preceptee is managing time appropriately.

Answers to Questions for Chapter Six:
Facilitating Adult Learning and a Variety of Learning Styles

Questions to Guide Your Learning

1. Your preceptee has had three patients who had particularly challenging behavior management problems. With each patient, she analyzed factors that seemed to underlie the patients' behaviors and then found ways of interacting with the patients

in ways that stopped the patients' challenging actions. Has this person learned? What elements of the definition of learning are present or not present in this situation?

There is a change in behavior and as described it seems to be relatively permanent because the preceptee repeated the skill three times. The change seemed to be intentional. It occurred as a result of interaction with and experience with a challenging patient.

2. What is one preceptor strategy that applies each of Knowles' five principles of adult learning to the precepting situation?

    a. Related to wanting to be self-directing, any of the following: Collaborating with the preceptee to make plans for desired learning experiences. Another is gradually letting go of the degree of supervision and your control of the activities as you work with the preceptee.

    b. Related to needing to know or to be able to do something for role achievement, any one of the following: Help the preceptee see how learning something will help with achieving role performance. Show how what will be learned is applicable to the preceptee's work. For established learning objectives, be sure the preceptee understands how this applies to skill progression. Be sensitive to events in the preceptee's life that may interfere with participation and make adjustments. Avoid demeaning or criticizing approaches with your preceptee.

    c. Related to experiences providing resources for learning, any one of the following: Use the preceptee's past experiences when collaborating to plan for new learning. Encourage plans that facilitate progression by building on past experiences. In new situations, encourage reflection about similarities with past experiences. Relate something you know your preceptee has experienced to what is being learned now.

    d. Related to problem-solving approaches to learning and seeking experiences that are immediately applicable to real life, any one of the following: Provide for learning experiences that are most immediately useful to your preceptee. Add experiences that build skills in commonly occurring situations rather than those that occur infrequently. Use a problem-centered approach to facilitate learning, being sure your preceptee can relate usefulness of what is to be learned to current or anticipated problems. Use discussion and questioning to prompt thinking and problem solving. Try to provide for application of learned experiences soon after learning-involved concepts are introduced. Provide feedback on performance as soon after application of something you instructed.

    e. Related to internal motivation factors, any one of the following: Provide feedback and positive reinforcement about what is being learned. Establish an environment of trust. Promote the preceptee's feeling of adequacy, competency, and security. Minimize barriers to learning.

3. What are two characteristics of each of Kolb's four learning styles?

    a. Diverging style: Takes in information through concrete experiences, likes to work with others, and processes experiences through reflective observation. Likes gathering information and generating differing ideas. Does not focus on taking action.

    b. Converging style: Takes in information through abstract conceptualization. Rather than reflecting, this learner takes action. Prefers working alone, focuses on solving a problem and finding a solution rather than thinking of possibilities and consequences extensively.

    c. Accommodator style: Takes in information through specific (hands-on) experiences and processes it through active experimentation. Likes to act, to carry out plans, may solve problems by intuition or trying out different approaches rather than using logical analysis. Takes risks.

    d. Assimilator style: Takes in information by abstract conceptualization, is good at organizing many ideas into an integrated whole, and likes things to be logically precise, with everything fitting together. This learner likes learning alone.

4. In Kolb's and Felder's learning style models, what is the importance of preferred learning strength?

    For those learners who have very strong preferences, learning from teachers who use opposing preference teaching strategies can be much more difficult, or at least slower. If the strength is not strong, there is a balance for learning through either opposing style. There tends not to be a problem.

5. What are the characteristics of each of Felder's four dimensions of learning preference?

    Each dimension consists of two opposing learning preferences.

    • Sensing and intuitive dimension: This dimension involves preferences for ways of perceiving information. Sensing learners like sights, sounds, active manipulation, concrete experiences, facts, and details. Intuitive learners prefer insights, ideas, memories, imagining, variety, innovation, and exploring ideas.

    • Visual and verbal dimension: This is another dimension that involves preferences for ways of perceiving information. Visual learners like pictures, diagrams, and demonstrations. Verbal learners have a greater preference for written and spoken words. These learners can easily take in information from verbal directions and lecture teaching strategies.

    • Active and reflective dimension: This dimension involves preferred ways of processing information. The active learner prefers processing by physical activity, manipulation, trying things out, and discussion. Reflective learners prefer processing more by thinking about or analyzing information.

    • Sequential and global dimension: Sequential learners prefer to progress in processing information using small progressive steps, and working with details.

Global learners prefer to process information by dealing with the big picture and seeing things holistically. Details may confuse this learner.

6. What is one preceptor strategy that would facilitate learning for each of Felder's four dimensions of learning styles?

   a. If your preceptee prefers to take in information by sensing, you may want to provide real-world experiences that involve seeing, hearing, or manipulating things. Provide concrete examples.

   b. If your preceptee prefers intuitive approaches, you may want to encourage the preceptee to explore various ideas or think of innovative approaches.

   c. If your preceptee prefers visual ways of taking in information, it would help if you provided demonstrations and drew diagrams and pictures.

   d. If your preceptee prefers verbal information over visual, then you may be able to merely give verbal directions. Visuals may confuse this learner.

   e. If your preceptee prefers active processing, try to provide active manipulation or discussion. Include concrete descriptions. Let the preceptee try things out and practice skills.

   f. If your preceptee prefers reflective processing, allow time for thinking about the information and for analyzing things. You might encourage reflective journaling. Be patient when it seems to be taking too long.

   g. If your preceptee prefers a sequential approach, try to break down the learning into steps. You may have to write out the steps so you don't jump around in explaining or demonstrating something.

   h. If your preceptee prefers global processing more, it would help if you provided an overview before dealing with details. Specific examples that illustrate how the materials can be used should also be helpful.

7. What are your learning style preferences and your preceptee's learning style preferences?

   There is, of course, no correct answer. Collaborate with your preceptee learner. You may provide input for your preceptee or the preceptee may provide you with insight about both of your learning styles. Encourage taking the Felder Learning Style Inventory online and then share results. Discuss approaches each of you might try to appeal to other dimensions by using more than one approach, approaches that would appeal to opposing dimensions.

Answers to Questions for Chapter Seven: Maintaining Your Preceptee's Motivation

Questions to Guide Your Learning

1. Why do you go to work? What motivates you to stay in a career that is fraught with challenges?

   The purpose of this question is to encourage you to reflect on what motivates you to remain in nursing. It is important for you to have internal motivators that sustain you through the difficult times when "money isn't enough." Make a list with two columns, "internal" and "external" motivators. List your values and beliefs about nursing under the internal motivators such as "help others" and "help improve one's quality of life." Under the external motivation column add things such as "money" and "flexible work days" (if this is true). When you are physically and emotionally exhausted, refer to the lists giving attention to the internal motivators that you listed.

2. What advice would you give someone who is thinking about entering into nursing?

   You are going to be asked the question a number of times in your professional career. Be clear on what you will say and speak from the heart.

3. What strategies could help you motivate a preceptee who is internally motivated to enter into or to remain in nursing?

   Remember that internal motivators are generally related to one's values system. So if you discover that your preceptee expresses concern about a patient's right to die, you may facilitate a learning experience in which your preceptee participates on the organization's or the unit's ethics committee. Aligning learning experiences that are congruent with one's values and beliefs may potentially strengthen internal motivators.

4. In what three ways do you plan to assist your preceptee achieve professional goals?

   Help your preceptee to divide large goals into smaller achievable subsets that are easily assessed. Encourage your preceptee to develop self-evaluation skills. The ability to self-evaluate provides feedback that will guide your preceptee's professional development for the duration of one's career. Create opportunities to enhance learning. Be vested in your preceptee's progress.

5. Your preceptee has a laundry list of things to be accomplished in a short period of time. You don't believe the list is achievable. What do you do?

   Enhance chances of success by helping your preceptee prioritize the list. Validate the length of time required to complete each of the tasks. Assess and reassess. The key point here is preventing your preceptee from floundering. Building on success one step at a time enhances motivation.

6. How will you create a clinical learning environment that is safe for your preceptee?

   Use skilled communication that is interactive. Engage your preceptee in discussions. Allow your preceptee to have the power and respect to participate collaboratively in planning, decision making, and when managing conflict. Create an environment of accountability. Share your experiences when planning, organizing, and assessing patient care. Doing so will help your preceptee develop an autonomous practice. Make appropriate assignments and expect your preceptee to provide high quality care. Give meaningful recognition. Reward your preceptee's positive contributions through ongoing feedback. You're a leader—be enthusiastic when role modeling professional practice.

7. What three things can you do to build autonomy in your preceptee?

Be consistent. Be objective and honest when providing feedback. Reinforce learning and provide positive recognition for a job well done. Facilitate experiences that build on prior knowledge. These are a few strategies that help build confidence in practice.

8. What will you do if your preceptee shares feelings of being incapable to complete a certain task?

Identify the motivation related to your preceptee's feelings. Is your preceptee unfamiliar with how the task is performed? Link the steps of the task to a similar situation that your preceptee feels confident in performing. Give feedback and encouragement. You may also want the preceptee to practice the task in a safe environment.

Answers to Questions for Chapter Eight: Working with Diversities

Questions to Guide Your Learning

1. What is the difference between culture, cultural competence, and cultural congruence?

Culture is the synthesis of beliefs, values, and customs of a particular group resulting in a pattern of behaviors. Cultural competence is the capacity to function in a particular way. It is the skill, knowledge and ability to contribute within the customs, beliefs, and values of a particular group. It is likely to be impossible to be culturally competent as there are as many cultures as there are individuals in the world. Cultural congruence recognizes that there are differences, sensitivities, and priorities that are specific to groups and individuals. Using this knowledge to engage in culturally diverse encounters is to interact with cultural congruence.

2. What are cultural artifacts? Is the culture of your organization reflective of what it is purported to be?

Cultural artifacts are things that characterize the culture. Most artifacts are observable such as dress code, the degree of formality found in communication and within an organizations structure. How decisions are made, formal and informal sources of support, rituals, myths, and stories describe the values of a culture.

Examine your organization's artifacts to establish the level of congruence between what the culture is said to be and what the culture actually reflects.

3. Where would organizational artifacts that represent the "real" culture be found?

One would be able to determine the actual culture through discussion and observation. Speaking with coworkers and observing "how things are done" are relevant strategies that reflect the actual culture.

4. What are four commonly occurring cultural differences?

Race, ethnicity, gender, age, religion, sexual orientation, mental or physical abilities, social class, and education level.

5. Using the model for developing cultural congruence, what four steps would you take to increase your cultural skills?

Four steps for developing cultural congruence include: developing cultural awareness, cultural knowledge, developing culturally congruent skills, and developing skills in managing cross-cultural encounters. Develop cultural awareness by knowing your own values and beliefs, biases and prejudices. Cultural knowledge is the process of understanding values, beliefs, and practices of culturally diverse groups. To develop congruent skills, one must develop empathy, trust, respect, and acceptance of cultural knowledge. Your preceptee's values and beliefs result from the sum of life's experiences. Each encounter is a product of cross-cultural interaction. Learn about your preceptee's life paradigm. Share your experiences, find similarities, and identify differences.

Use reflection to guide your future encounters.

6. How do "Baby Boomers," "Generation X," and "Nexters" value the concept of work?

Generally "Generation X" people try to maintain a balance between work and life. "Nexters" value life above work and "Baby Boomers" have a strong work ethic.

7. What three words would best describe "Baby Boomers"?

"Leaders," "Peacekeepers," and "Workaholics."

8. What is one characteristic that is shared between "Xers" and "Nexters"?

"Xers" and "Nexters" generally hold few biases and appreciate diversity.

9. What are two of the many challenges that internationally educated nurses experience when first working in the United States?

Language, cultural diversity, feelings of isolation, and working in a healthcare context that is radically different.

10. What are three preceptor strategies that might facilitate an internationally educated nurse preceptee's transition into professional practice?

Be aware that there are cultural differences. Analyze your preconceptions about your preceptee. Validate your perceptions by acquiring cultural knowledge through reading and communicating. Learn about the country from which your preceptee originated. Learn the political, economic, and social structures. Honor your preceptee's beliefs and values. Explain situations and validate perceptions. Reflect on your encounters with your preceptee and collaboratively review outcomes and strategies for improving your preceptee's professional practice.

Answers to Questions for Chapter Nine: Assessing Preceptee Progress: How Are We Doing?

Questions to Guide Your Learning

1. What is the difference between assessment and evaluation?

   Assessment involves observing for intended learning outcomes (what the learner knows and is able to do). Evaluation involves making judgments about the qualities of what was observed.

2. What will you assess about your preceptee?

   What he or she knows or is able to do and making decisions about how well these outcomes are occurring.

3. What are four processes used in assessing performance? How should your preceptee be involved in these processes?

   • Developing clear goals and objectives (outcomes you want to see)

   • Observing or measuring for desired outcomes

   • Making judgments about observations

   • Working to improve behaviors

   The preceptee should collaborate with you in each of these assessment processes.

4. In what way should you use objectives when assessing your preceptee's performance?

   Objectives should guide what the preceptor and preceptee do to achieve them. They should guide your observations for outcomes and decisions you make about how well the outcomes are being achieved. In other words, they are the basis for all processes of assessment.

5. What is the best timing for giving performance feedback? What is the purpose of providing for feedback about the preceptee's performance?

   The best timing for giving feedback is as soon as possible after observing something.

   Sharing observations provides an opportunity to clarify and verify observations and perceptions. It also allows the opportunity and time to improve behavior.

6. How might stakeholders influence the assessment process? How can you involve them in the process?

   They may be involved in providing information about preceptee outcomes. They may also have responsibilities for assessing the preceptee. Because they will be working with the preceptee after the precepted experience ends, they may be involved in accepting or rejecting the preceptee. They may have wanted different outcomes than you established and be dissatisfied with the preceptee's outcomes. They may resent or disapprove of the time you spend with the preceptee.

It would be important to include them in either developing or approving the intended outcomes of the experience. They should also be involved in making decisions about any changes that will be made in how you work with the team. Involve them in periodic summaries of preceptee progress. Ask for their observations of preceptee performance. If they will be involved in evaluating the preceptee, share your observations and judgments about performance periodically.

7. What are the differences between goals and objectives?

Goals tend to be more global, indicating major outcomes at the end of a learning experience. Objectives specifically spell out the achievement behaviors that describe the ending outcomes.

8. What do objectives describe?

- What the preceptee should know and be able to do
- Outcomes, not processes, used to achieve the outcomes
- Observable measurable behaviors
- Student, not teacher, behaviors

9. What are three components of useful objectives?

Observable behavior, circumstances under which the preceptee demonstrates intended behaviors, and expected standards that describe how well the preceptee demonstrates intended outcomes.

10. What should the observable behavior component of an objective describe?

- An observable behavior that indicates the learner has achieved the intended outcome. If the behavior is not observable (covert), a behavior that indicates the desired outcome should be described.
- A main desired behavior.

11. What are factors that could be described in expected standards?

Expected standards describe how well the behaviors should be performed. They may describe factors such as speed, accuracy, quantity, specific qualities, or minimum critical behaviors.

12. What are three recommendations for facilitating psychomotor skill development?

- Consider the frequency and complexity of the skill to be developed and move from simple to complex.
- Deal with background information and scientific rationale before practicing or demonstrating a procedure rather than during the performance.
- Provide a model of the desired behaviors—written directions, pictures, video, or demonstration.

- If the skill is complex, break it down into smaller sets of skills and allow learner to master each set before adding the next set of steps.
- Encourage mental rehearsal.
- During initial return, demonstrations offer feedback guidance during the performance.
- After return demonstrations and practicing, let the learner fully concentrate on the procedure. Do not interrupt or discuss behaviors.
- Provide opportunities for practice.
- Provide for reflection about performance.

13. Who should be involved in planning for achieving objectives?

    All stakeholders, the preceptee, you the preceptor, and anyone involved in making decisions about outcomes.

14. What are examples of preceptor behaviors that interfere with preceptee learning?

    - Being unavailable for conferencing, assistance, or advice when needed.
    - Placing the preceptee in situations for which he or she has no preparation or experience.
    - Placing the preceptee in situations they are unable to manage.
    - Over-supervising or under-supervising.
    - Belittling the preceptee.
    - Criticizing the preceptee in front of others.
    - Withholding information.
    - Trying to trick or catch the preceptee in making a mistake.

15. How would you tell your preceptee that something he or she has done does not meet expectations?

    In a calm nonthreatening demeanor, check the preceptee's perception of the event or behavior. Share your objective observations with the preceptee. Clarify perceptions. Discuss with the preceptee his or her thinking and rationale for the behavior and your rationale as well. Either you or the preceptee or both of you should describe what should happen in the future as well as anything that may need to happen to facilitate planned changes. It would be wise to project a timeline for expected changes as well.

16. How will your teaching vary because of your preceptee's learning style?

    Look at the strategies suggested in Chapter 6. Try to use a strategy that fosters your preceptee's learning. For example, if your preceptee seems to like things in writing, try to do that rather than using only verbal approaches. If you like details and then the big picture but your preceptor needs the big picture before seeing the details, try to stretch a bit and start with an overview then the details. If you cannot, the learner will still learn. It just may be more of a struggle.

17. How will you involve your preceptee in self-assessment? In assessing your precepting behaviors?

Start from the beginning to encourage the preceptee to reflect about his or her thinking and actions. If you are noncritical and constructive in conversations and encourage this reflection consistently, you should develop a habit of facilitating the preceptee's self-evaluation. The same would be true of your precepting behaviors. Reflect about them and discuss them with your preceptee and peers.

18. How would you react in the following situations:

- You note that one of your preceptee's patients is more acutely ill than the others and you have discussed this with the preceptee. You see that the preceptee has checked medications and is assessing other patients before going into the sicker patient's room.

  Check your perceptions with the preceptee and ask about thinking. Ask questions of the preceptee about potential consequences of delaying assessment. Ask him or her to propose a change in priorities. Share you reasoning with the preceptee.

- Your preceptee is giving a very disorganized patient report. The preceptee leaves out quite a few vital points, and keeps looking through her notes to find report items so report lasts a long time.

  Again, check the preceptee's thinking and perceptions. Perhaps he or she had some late shift problems you didn't know about. Perhaps you and the preceptee have not yet discussed how to do an appropriate report. Ask the preceptee to develop a list of what should be included in a report and how to organize it. Before report time ask the preceptee to go over report plans. Help him or her think through what would be important and to anticipate what the next shift would need to know. Have him or her report to you first.

- Your preceptee is not a self-starter. She waits for you to tell her to try doing a new procedure. You would like her to jump in and offer to do this on her own, without your prompting or pushing her to get the experience.

  This is possibly due to your preceptee's low confidence level. You might start by having the preceptee develop a list of procedures he or she needs to practice because these procedures are common on the unit. You can add some to the list if necessary. You might then suggest how you will proceed in helping (pointing out a nonthreatening approach such as verbal rehearsal, or you demonstrating the procedure before the preceptee does it). Ask the preceptee to look for opportunities to practice the procedure. Suggest that he or she let other nurses on the team know that he or she would like to be able to do the procedure. By all means, be sure the preceptee is supported during these experiences.

- A patient tells you that the preceptee makes her nervous. The patient says the preceptee doesn't seem to know how to operate the intravenous pump.

You might share the patient's comment with the preceptee. It may not be quite true. Or the preceptee may be thinking he or she should know how to use the pump and is reluctant to ask for help. Away from the patient, demonstrate the pump or ask the preceptee if there is some aspect that he or she is confused about and demonstrate that or help the preceptee troubleshoot the pump functions (only if preceptee seems comfortable enough to proceed).

19. Which of the following sample learning objectives contains all the elements of effective objectives (add characteristics that make the objective effective if it is lacking one or more elements)?

- Understands two purposes of writing anecdotal notes in assessing skill progression.

   Observable behavior—Add an indicator for understands. "Understands (verbally describes)."

   Behavior circumstances—none indicated but probably not needed.

   Expected standards—Two purposes are indicated. Could add appropriate purposes but that would be implied.

- Given the assignment of four patients, accurately lists in priority order the degree to which those patients are in jeopardy of rapidly becoming more critically ill.

   Observable behavior—list. This is not the main intent of the objective. The main intent is prioritize potential jeopardy (lists in priority order).

   Behavior circumstances—The learner can do this for four patients.

   Expected standards—Accurately; this might be a bit fuzzy, however.

- Knows the rationale for checking gastric residual in patients being fed via a nasogastric tube.

   Observable behavior—knows but this is not observable. "Verbally describes" would be observable.

   Behavior circumstances—a patient receiving a nasogastric tube feeding.

   Expected standards—None noted. Could say "Accurately describes (states) three rationale without error" ("accurately" and "without error" are the expected standards).

- Given three Chem-6 lab results, selects (verbally) those results that are in the abnormal range without error.

   Observable behavior—Knows with the added indicator of "verbally selects."

   Behavior circumstances—given three Chem-6 lab results.

   Expected standards—without error.

Answers to Questions for Chapter Ten: Launching the Precepting Experience and Tracking Progress

Questions to Guide Your Learning

1. What are five roles you will perform as you precept?
   - Coach—to direct and to guide the learner
   - Teacher—to manage the learning opportunities
   - Facilitator—to maximize outcomes through guidance and supervision
   - Resource person—to help the preceptee discover the people, equipment, or material used to perform a project or a task
   - Evaluator—to assess the preceptee's progress and level of achievement

2. What are four legal considerations you should attend to as a preceptor?
   - Your liability while working with the preceptee.
   - That the preceptor is responsible for appropriate supervision and appropriate assignments.
   - Know the preceptee's permitted tasks, tasks that require certification, and tasks not permitted by the agency or school of nursing.
   - If working with a student, ensure presence of liability insurance, a signed contract, that the student is currently registered at the school of nursing, and that there are completed appropriate immunizations and health clearances.

3. What is your liability when working with a preceptee?

   Both the preceptor and preceptee are held accountable for behaviors expected of a person with a license or those of a student at a particular level in an education program. You are liable for adequate supervision and for appropriately assigning responsibilities and activities.

4. What will most affect your decision to assign patients to your preceptee?

   Assessing the preceptee's capabilities and carefully supervising his or her abilities to ensure appropriate assignment.

5. What key personnel will you want to introduce to your preceptee early in the precepting experience?
   - Initially, you want to introduce the preceptee to the people with whom they will be working. Who are your coworkers? Nurses, administrative assistants, unit manager, unlicensed assistive personnel, and, of course, the physicians who admit patients to your unit.
   - As your preceptee becomes familiar with the unit personnel, begin introductions to administrative officers and personnel from ancillary departments that support your unit.

6. Your preceptee has just graduated from a basic nursing program. He exhibits common beginner behaviors. Choose three beginner behaviors, and describe how you will work with each.

- Routines tend to determine behaviors

    Collaborate with the preceptee at the beginning of the shift and periodically throughout the shift to assess the preceptee's planning and to identify appropriate prioritization and organization.

- Has problems with prioritizing

    Proceed the same as for the behavior above. Assist as necessary to help the preceptee prioritize and organize in ways that involve the patient's status rather than just routines consisting primarily of things to get done.

- Has problems planning for patients' progression and anticipating patient responses

    Without much repetitive experience it is difficult to estimate the time required to complete a procedure. It is also challenging to anticipate variations in a patient's condition. You can provide needed information (or help the preceptee find the information), help with anticipating future events, and encourage reflection about the situation. By reflecting, the preceptee can discover similarities between current and previous cases which makes it more likely the beginner will recall events and apply learning in new situations with decreasing need for help from you.

- Focuses on isolated pieces of information rather than an organized whole

    You may need to help the preceptee attend to what is salient in a situation. Discuss events with the preceptee that highlight what is salient. Help the beginner make meaning of all the disjointed pieces of information that have been perceived.

- Unexpected events, events that disrupt routines may cause the preceptee to become "frozen," and unable to complete meaningful activities

    It is beneficial to focus on one thing for a moment, deal with one step at a time, stop and plan what to do. You might suggest to the beginner that if this happens, to consult with you or go to a room where he or she can concentrate for a minute about what to do first. Sometimes if you suggest one initial action, the beginner will become "unfrozen" and continue with sound actions without additional prompting.

- Uses extensive memory aids

    Encourage this activity. Suggest that the preceptee either use or develop a worksheet that will help with remembering details. It may also be a source of information for you as you assess preceptee progress.

- Lacks confidence; asks numerous questions

    Be supportive. Suggest actions the preceptee may try rather than describing what they should not do. Try to anticipate and prevent performance problems. In rapidly changing patient situations it is beneficial to help your preceptee complete some of the patient care tasks while coaching thinking about rationale for changes in the patient's condition and resulting responses. Refrain from completely taking over the care of the patient.

- Generates limited hypotheses about patient status; does not verify hypotheses

  Help the beginner generate possible causes or explanations for patient conditions. Ask questions that stimulate thinking about possibilities. Help validate hypotheses, finding ways of ruling them in or out. Help your preceptee discover answers whenever possible. Ask questions like, "What else could explain what you are seeing" or "What else might you try" or "What else do you need to know about what is happening?"

7. Organization is a problem when someone is new to a situation. What is one strategy you might use to help your preceptee organize at the beginning of a shift?

   Help the preceptee determine priorities and then organize to respond to them. Check progress periodically during the shift to determine plans and organization. Assist with anticipating events that may interfere with or alter organization. Encourage the preceptee to seek your help if he or she is having trouble with keeping on time and meeting priorities. If the preceptee needs help and delegation is appropriate, help the preceptee discover appropriate ways to delegate.

8. What is a preceptor strategy that applies to the following principle of adult learning: readiness to learn is influenced by the need to know or be able to do something?

   - Help the preceptee make the connection between what you might be teaching and a clear view of how learning this will help in role performance.

   - Clarify that what will be learned is applicable to roles being developed. You could just tell preceptees how they will use a piece of information. You could also help the preceptee discover what knowledge is needed. Ask the preceptee how the information you are providing might be used.

   - If you and the preceptee have established an objective for the next shift, be sure the preceptee understands how this applies to skill progression, how doing this will help increase skills.

   - Be sensitive to the possibility that your preceptee's current responsibilities and living background events may affect learning readiness and the quality of participation in learning activities.

9. Your preceptee is an assimilator, whereas you are an accommodator. What is one potential problem in working with this preceptee?

   This preceptee may prefer to work alone and to be more independent than you would like. Discuss your need for more observation and collaboration with the preceptee. There will be a preference for thinking things through and wanting to fit details into an integrated whole picture. There could be a reluctance to take action. Your preceptee may need to understand detailed rationale for some procedures. You, on the other hand, don't focus on these details, you may have known them way back, but you have not used them in awhile. You could assist your preceptee in looking up and discussing details and rationale. Both of you may need to make changes or be tolerant and understanding of your differences. You could also use each others' differences. You could encourage the preceptee to take action more readily while your preceptee may make you hesitate, ask questions about some potential problems you hadn't considered before you take some action. Keep in mind that both of you may have weak learning preferences and there may be no problem.

10. The preceptee may be motivated to learn but may have some anxiety about the clinical experience. How will you help the preceptee gain confidence and maintain motivation?

- Help your preceptee set small proximal goals that are easily attainable. Collaborate with the preceptee to determine the steps necessary to achieve the goals.
- Encourage your preceptee to engage in self-assessment. Help the preceptee reevaluate and modify goals as needed.
- Give positive feedback that guides the preceptee toward success.
- Celebrate and reward success with enthusiasm.
- Remember, progress enhances self-efficacy and self-efficacy is critical to developing and maintaining motivation.

11. What are six components that create a safe learning environment within the complex environment of health care?

- Skilled communication
- Effective decision making
- True collaboration
- Appropriate assignments
- Meaningful recognition
- Authentic leadership

12. Your preceptee is culturally different from you. What three things can you do to enhance your cultural awareness?

- You may first want to complete a cultural self-assessment to indicate your values, beliefs, and practices.
- Accept your biases and understand that you may have cultural preconceptions regarding your preceptee. Communicate with your preceptee. Becoming knowledgeable on a personal basis may help you to avoid misconceptions.
- Understand that each individual is a product of life's experiences. Learn about the context of the preceptee. Try to find commonalities and explore differences.

13. The preceptor is a "Baby Boomer" and the preceptee is a "Nexter." Even though the work day is complete you notice the preceptor remains on the unit to chat with a physician as the preceptee leaves to attend Pilates class. What are two examples of generational diversity shown in this scenario?

- "Baby Boomers" generally believe that the work is never done as they are perceived as workaholics. While "Nexters" enjoy working, their preference is to enjoy their lifestyle.
- "Baby Boomers" love to communicate using lots of details. They enjoy collaboration. "Nexters," on the other hand, are action oriented. They strive for achievement and quickly move on when the job is complete.

14. What are four strategies you can use to assess your preceptee's performance?

Any four of the following:

- Observation of preceptee's behaviors—procedures, care plans, documentation, reflection, etc.
- Observation of preceptee demonstration of a technical skill
- Using a checklist of critical behaviors to facilitate observations of technical procedures
- Analysis of anecdotal notes, looking for patterns of behavior and improvements
- Analyzing preceptee's journal reflections, assessing for new or improved cognitive or behavior skills
- Discussions or conferences, assessing for insights and new or improved behaviors
- Questioning about preceptee planning or thinking
- Observing abilities while using role play

15. Your student preceptee is quiet. She asks almost no questions, and she makes many mistakes in performing procedures even though you have repeatedly helped her with the procedures. What are three actions you should take if you believe she should not pass the precepted experience?

Any three of the actions below:

- Collaborate with your preceptee to identify and verify expected outcomes. Plan for ways to achieve these outcomes.
- Work to prevent failure. As soon as you see behaviors that are unacceptable, discuss your observations with the preceptee. Encourage the preceptee to explain the behaviors. Work with the preceptee to solve problems. Make plans for specific ways to improve behaviors. This allows time for remediation. If you wait until near the end of the experience, it may be too late to fix the behaviors.
- If the preceptee is a student, involve the faculty in the school of nursing as soon as you recognize a problematic performance.
- Keep anecdotal notes to specifically describe unacceptable behaviors. Be as objective as possible.
- Be sure you are neither too strict nor too lenient in your evaluations.

APPENDIX B

Template of Agency Contract for Student Precepted Experiences

CLINICAL INTERNSHIP AGREEMENT

This Agreement is between _____ [type of entity: e.g., hospital name or corporation] ("Facility") and _____ University ("University"), and is effective as of _____ [date]

    A.   Facility owns and operates a general acute care hospital and/or skilled nursing facility and/or various outpatient clinics.

    B.   University operates fully accredited health sciences programs offering degrees in nursing, physical therapy, and (list other programs).

    C.   The parties will both benefit by making a clinical training program ("Program") available to University students at the Facility.

The parties agree as follows:

  I.   GENERAL INFORMATION ABOUT THE PROGRAM

    A.   The maximum number of University students who may participate in the Program during each training period shall be mutually agreed by the parties at least 30 days before the training period begins.

    B.   The starting date and length of each program training period shall be determined by mutual agreement.

  II.   UNIVERSITY'S RESPONSIBILITIES

    A.   **Student Profiles.** University shall advise each student enrolled in the Program to complete and send to Facility a student profile which shall include the student's name, address, and telephone number. Each student shall be responsible for submitting his or her student profile before the Program training period begins. Hospital shall regard this information as confidential and shall use the information only to identify each student.

    B.   **Schedule of Assignments.** University shall notify Facility's Clinical Coordinator of student assignments, including the name of the student, level of academic preparation, and length and dates of proposed clinical experience.

    C.   **Program Coordinator.** University shall designate a faculty member to coordinate with Hospital's designee in planning the Program to be provided to students.

    D.   **Orientation Program.** Facility shall provide for orientation to the faculty and to students at the beginning of their enrollment in the Program.

    E.   **Records.** University shall maintain all personnel records for its staff and all academic records for its students.

    F.   **Student Responsibilities.** University shall notify students in the Program that they are responsible for:

      1. Complying with Facility's clinical and administrative policies, procedures, rules, and regulations;

2. Arranging for transportation and living arrangements if not provided by University;

3. Assuming responsibility for their personal illnesses, necessary immunizations, tuberculin tests, and annual health examinations;

4. Maintaining the confidentiality of patient information.

   a. No student shall have access to or have the right to receive any medical record, except when necessary in the regular course of the clinical experience. The discussion, transmission, or narration in any form by students of any individually identifiable patient information, medical or otherwise, obtained in the course of the Program is forbidden except as a necessary part of the practical experience. [REQUIRED PROVISION/HIPAA]

   b. Neither University nor its employees or agents shall be granted access to individually identifiable information unless the patient has first given consent using a form approved by Facility that complies with applicable state and federal law, including the Health Insurance Portability and Accountability Act ("HIPAA") and its implementing regulations. [REQUIRED PROVISION/HIPAA]

   c. Facility shall reasonably assist University in obtaining patient consent in appropriate circumstances. In the absence of consent, students shall use de-identified information only in any discussions about the clinical experience with University, its employees, or agents. [REQUIRED PROVISION/HIPAA]

5. Complying with Facility's dress code and wearing name badges identifying themselves as students;

6. Attending an orientation to be provided by the Facility;

7. Notifying Facility immediately of any violation of state or federal laws by any student;

8. Providing services to Facility's patients only under the direct supervision of Facility's professional staff;

9. Student shall sign Waiver and Hold Harmless Agreement (Exhibit A) and provide the signed agreement to the Facility prior to beginning the clinical internship program.

G. **Payroll Taxes and Withholdings.** University shall be solely responsible for any payroll taxes, withholdings, workers' compensation, and any other insurance or benefits of any kind for University's employees and agents, if any, who provide services to the Program under this Agreement. Students are not employees or agents of the University and shall receive no compensation for their participation in the Program, either from University or Facility. For purposes of this agreement, however, students are trainees and shall be considered members of Facility's "work force" as that term is defined by the

HIPAA regulations at 45 C.F.R. § 160.103. [PRIOR SENTENCE IS REQUIRED PROVISION/HIPAA] University / Facility shall bear all costs associated with providing workers' compensation coverage for them.

III. FACILITY'S RESPONSIBILITIES

A. **Clinical Experience.** Facility shall accept from University the mutually agreed upon number of students enrolled in the Program and shall provide the students with supervised clinical experience.

B. **Facility Designee.** Facility shall designate a member of its staff to participate with University's designee in planning, implementing, and coordinating the Program.

C. **Access to Facilities.** Facility shall permit students enrolled in the Program access to Facility resources as appropriate and necessary for their Program, provided that the students' presence shall not interfere with Facility's activities.

D. **Records and Evaluations.** Facility shall maintain complete records and reports on each student's performance and provide an evaluation to University on forms the University shall provide.

E. **Withdrawal of Students.** Facility may request that University withdraw from the program any student who Facility determines is not performing satisfactorily, refuses to follow Facility's administrative policies, procedures, rules, and regulations, or violates any federal or state laws. Such requests must be in writing and must include a statement as to the reason or reasons for Facility's request. University shall comply with the written request within five (5) days after actually receiving it.

F. **Emergency Health Care/First Aid.** Facility shall, on any day when a student is receiving training at its facilities, provide to that student necessary emergency health care or first aid for accidents occurring in its facilities. Except as provided in this paragraph, Facility shall have no obligation to furnish medical or surgical care to any student. Students have the financial responsibility for costs incurred in any such care. Students shall be responsible for procuring and maintaining their own health insurance at their own expense. Students shall provide Facility with evidence of said health insurance.

G. **Student Supervision.** Facility shall permit students to perform services for patients only when under the supervision of a registered, licensed, or certified clinician/professional on Facility's staff. Such clinicians or professionals are to be certified or licensed in the discipline in which supervision is provided. Students shall work, perform assignments, and participate in facility activities and programs at the discretion of their Facility-designated supervisors. Students are to be regarded as trainees, not employees, and are not to replace Facility's staff. [REQUIRED PROVISION/HIPAA]

H. **Facility's Confidentiality Policies.** As trainees, students shall be considered members of Facility's "work force," as that term is defined by the HIPAA regulations at 45 C.F.R. § 160.103, and shall be subject to Facility's policies respecting confidentiality of medical information. In order to ensure that students comply with such policies, Facility shall provide students with substantially the same training that it provides to its regular employees or insure that the training provided by the University meets all its requirements. [REQUIRED PROVISION/HIPAA]

IV. AFFIRMATIVE ACTION AND NONDISCRIMINATION

The parties agree that all students receiving clinical training pursuant to this Agreement shall be selected without discrimination on account of race, color, religion, national origin, ancestry, disability, marital status, gender, gender identity, sexual orientation, age, or veteran status.

V. STATUS OF UNIVERSITY AND FACILITY

The parties expressly understand and agree that the students enrolled in the Program are in attendance for educational purposes, and such students are not considered employees of either Facility or University for any purpose, including, but not limited to compensation for services, welfare and pension benefits, or workers' compensation insurance. Students are, however, considered members of Facility's "work force" for purposes of HIPAA compliance. [REQUIRED PROVISION/HIPAA]

VI. INSURANCE

A. It is agreed and recognized that the University is a self-insured public agency of the State of _____. Accordingly, the self-insured and public agency status of the University provides sufficient evidence of financial ability to respond to any insurance obligation. Accordingly, no insurance certificates or endorsements shall be required. The University shall maintain and provide evidence of workers' compensation and disability coverage as required by law. Note this would be changed to accurately describe the educational institution.

B. **Student Insurance.** Student shall procure and maintain in force during the term of the student's internship, at the student's sole cost and expense, professional liability insurance in amounts reasonably necessary to protect the student against liability arising from any and all negligent acts or incidents caused by the student. Coverage under such professional liability insurance shall be not less than one million dollars ($1,000,000) for each occurrence and three million dollars ($3,000,000) in the aggregate. Such coverage is to be obtained from an insurer rated A or better by AM Best. Student shall be required to provide evidence of his or her professional liability coverage to Facility.

C. **Facility Insurance.** Facility shall procure and maintain in force during the term of this Agreement, at its sole cost and expense, insurance in amounts that are reasonably necessary to protect it against liability arising from any and all negligent acts or incidents caused by its employees. Coverage under such professional and commercial general liability insurance shall be not less than one million dollars ($1,000,000) for each occurrence and three million dollars ($3,000,000) in the aggregate. Such coverage is to be obtained from an insurer rated A or better by AM Best or a qualified program of self-insurance. Facility shall also maintain and provide evidence of workers' compensation and disability coverage for its employees as required by law.

VII. INDEMNIFICATION.

A. University agrees to indemnify, defend, and hold harmless Facility and its affiliates, directors, trustees, officers, agents, and employees against all claims, demands, damages, costs, expenses of whatever nature, including court costs and reasonable attorney's fees, arising out of or resulting from University's negligence, or in proportion to the University's comparative fault.

B. Facility agrees to indemnify, defend, and hold harmless University and its affiliates, directors, trustees, officers, agents, and employees against all claims, demands, damages, costs, expenses of whatever nature, including court costs and reasonable attorney's fees, arising out of or resulting from Facility's negligence, or in proportion to the Facility's comparative fault.

VIII. TERM AND TERMINATION

A. **Term.** This Agreement shall be effective as of the date first written above and shall remain in effect for _____ years, terminating on _____.

B. **Renewal.** This Agreement may be renewed by mutual agreement.

C. **Termination.** This Agreement may be terminated at any time by written agreement or upon 30 days' advance written notice by one party to the other, PROVIDED, HOWEVER, that in no event shall termination take effect with respect to currently enrolled students, who shall be permitted to complete their training for any semester in which termination would otherwise occur.

IX. GENERAL PROVISIONS

A. **Amendments.** In order to ensure compliance with HIPAA, the following provisions of this Agreement shall not be subject to amendment by any means during the term of this Agreement or any extensions: Section II, Paragraph F, subdivisions 4.a), 4.b), and 4.c); Section II, Paragraph G, to the extent it provides that students are members of Hospital's "work force" for purposes of HIPAA; Section III, Paragraphs H and I; and Section V. This Agreement may otherwise be amended at any time by mutual agreement of the parties without additional consideration, provided that before any amendment shall take effect, it shall be reduced to writing and signed by the parties.

B. **Assignment.** Neither party shall voluntarily or by operation of law, assign or otherwise transfer this Agreement without the other party's prior written consent. Any purported assignment in violation of this paragraph shall be void.

C. **Captions.** Captions and headings in this Agreement are solely for the convenience of the parties, are not a part of this Agreement, and shall not be used to interpret or determine the validity of this Agreement or any of its provisions.

D. **Counterparts.** This Agreement may be executed in any number of counterparts, each of which shall be deemed an original, but all such counterparts together shall constitute one and the same instrument.

E. **Entire Agreement.** This Agreement is the entire agreement between the parties. No other agreements, oral or written, have been entered into with respect to the subject matter of this Agreement.

F. **Governing Law.** The validity, interpretation, and performance of this Agreement shall be governed by and construed in accordance with the laws of the State of _____.

G. **Notices.** Notices required under this Agreement shall be sent to the parties by certified or registered mail, return receipt requested, postage prepaid, at the addresses set forth below:

TO UNIVERSITY: _____

Attn: _____

TO FACILITY: _____

Attn: _____

X. EXECUTION

By signing below, each of the following represent that they have authority to execute this Agreement and to bind the party on whose behalf their signature is made.

UNIVERSITY   FACILITY

By _____   By _____

Name _____   Name _____

Title _____   Title _____

Date _____   Date _____

EXHIBIT A

WAIVER AND HOLD HARMLESS AGREEMENT

I, _____ hereby state, represent and agree that:

1. I am over eighteen years of age.

2. I am a student enrolled at (name of university) and, as such, I am participating in the University's clinical internship program at

   _____ (herein the "Facility").

3. I acknowledge that I am neither eligible for nor entitled to workers' compensation benefits under the University or Facility's coverage based upon my participation in the program.

4. I hereby waive, discharge, release, hold harmless, and indemnify the Facility, its employees, officers, agents, and representatives from any and all liability, losses, or damages of any nature or cause to any persons or property, including the undersigned, arising out of, or during, my participation in the clinical internship program.

I have read the foregoing; I understand and agree to the terms therein. I recognize that as consideration for agreeing to said terms the Facility will permit me to participate in the clinical experience program at the Facility.

Dated: _____

                              Signature of Student

                              _____

                              Typed Name of Student

APPENDIX C

Template of Preceptor Contract for Student Nurses

[NAME OF SCHOOL OF NURSING]

Student Contract for Precepted Clinical Learning Experiences

Student _____   Phone _____

Faculty Liaison _____   Phone _____

Preceptor _____   Phone _____

Agency _____   Phone _____

Unit in Agency _____   Phone _____

Nurse Manager _____   Phone _____

Dates of clinical experiences From_____   To _____

Shift _____

Overall Goal of Clinical Experience:

To develop and improve my clinical and professional skills by providing holistic professional nursing care considering patients, families, and communities within the scope of my practice through interaction with an assigned preceptor at the level of a beginning professional nurse in an assigned clinical setting.

Objectives:

By the end of clinical practicum hours, there will be evidence that I will
[Insert your clinical objectives]

_____

_____

_____

_____

_____

_____

Signatures:

Student _____   Date _____

Preceptor _____   Date _____

Faculty _____   Date _____

You must meet with your clinical faculty advisor and preceptor to sign this contract before you clinical experience may begin.

Enter Your Personal and Unit-Specific Objectives

PARTICIPANT RESPONSIBILITIES

Agency Responsibilities

1. Identifies the key contact person in the agency who is responsible for coordinating the preceptor program with the University.
2. Identifies, with the assistance of the instructor, qualified preceptors (BSN prepared and having completed a Preceptor Training Program, and 2 years employment in agency).
3. Provides each student with the clinical experiences necessary to meet his or her learning objectives.
4. Participates in evaluation of total preceptorship program.

Student Responsibilities

1. Analyzes and determines what he or she wants to gain from the experience and elaborates and prioritizes specific learning objectives to meet specific needs (with guidance from faculty and preceptor).
2. Analyzes and determines appropriate priorities to complete the course-required learning activities.
3. With preceptor, discusses reciprocal expectations and devises a tentative schedule of activities to meet the learning objectives.
4. Seeks supervision and feedback from preceptor on an ongoing basis.
5. Schedules an initial and weekly conference with preceptor to review and evaluate objectives and activities, even if daily contact occurs.
6. Plans agenda for weekly conferences with preceptor.
7. Maintains a daily log regarding, describing, and analyzing aspects of the experience.
8. Performs within the administrative framework of the agency.
9. Achieves clinical objectives.
10. Informs instructor, preceptor and agency immediately if unable to meet commitments due to illness or other reasons; sick days will be made up.
11. Provides instructor with proof of professional malpractice insurance, CPR certification, completion of all health clearances, and current TB skin test.
12. Informs preceptor and instructor of any problems that arise during the placement in a timely manner.
13. Conducts a self-evaluation according to the clinical objectives.
14. Maintains communication with preceptor and agency personnel to ensure continuity of care.

15. Participates with preceptor and instructor in completing the clinical assignments for clinical conference.

16. Participates in joint conferences with preceptor and instructor as scheduled.

17. Participates in clinical experiences only under the guidance of assigned clinical preceptor.

Faculty Responsibilities

1. Selects learning facilities that can provide positive learning experiences.

2. Assists agency to identify qualified preceptors using established criteria.

3. In collaboration with agency, determines where students will be placed.

4. Initiates contact and maintains communication with the preceptor to clarify student, instructor, and agency roles, learning objectives, etc., throughout the semester.

5. Provides agency and preceptor with a copy of the course description, learning objectives, dates of beginning and ending of the experience, and the number of hours required. Facilitates and monitors total clinical experience.

6. Is available for consultation with preceptor, agency, and student.

7. Approves student's specific learning objectives.

8. Provides individual supervision of students to assist in meeting learning objectives on a regularly scheduled basis.

9. Evaluates students according to learning objectives, in collaboration with agency preceptor, using evaluation form provided by instructor.

10. Visits each clinical placement on a periodic basis.

11. Conducts evaluation conferences with preceptor and student at the end of the semester.

12. Reviews student's daily log weekly to provide feedback to student.

13. Documents that each student is covered by professional liability insurance, required immunizations, current TB skin test or x-ray, completed health clearance, and current CPR certification.

14. Determines student's grade for the experience.

Preceptor Responsibilities

1. Serves as clinical expert, role model, and direct supervisor of student.

2. Meets with student initially and throughout experience at predetermined times to review and reevaluate objectives and activities even if daily contact occurs.

3. With student, jointly plans and arranges assignments, projects, and activities to meet the learning objectives within designated time frames.

4. Encourages student to be increasingly self-directed.

5. Shares experiences and knowledge to develop student's abilities and confidence.

6. Allows students to provide direct patient care to meet objectives.

7. Gives feedback to student on an ongoing basis.

8. Participates in the site visits made by the instructor.

9. Informs the instructor immediately of any problems arising from the student's placement.

10. Using the form provided, evaluates the student's progress in meeting his or her objectives, in collaboration with the instructor.

Faculty and Student Orientation Plan

It is the program's responsibility under the terms of the formal contractual agreement to provide for/facilitate an orientation of student and faculty assigned to the agency. Orientation will be collaboratively developed with agency representative and within the context of the roles and responsibilities delineated above. Students and faculty, as necessary, will be oriented before commencement of clinical learning experiences for a given semester.

Index

NOTES

NOTES

NOTES

NOTES

NOTES

NOTES

NOTES